# A YEAR OF MR. LUCKY

a memoir of submission, loss, & longing

## MEG WEBER

"I'm thrilled with how this memoir inhabits the form of the epistolary novel and fills it with contemporary digital communication and transgressive content. To bring kink to the foreground is to insist on a radical kind of present tense, an unapologetic desire and desiring body. Which is to say that this book is a political act where the story of desire, loss, power, pleasure, pain and standing up take on phenomenal new meanings."
    – Lidia Yuknavitch, author of *The Chronology of Water*

"A portrait of longing so vivid and agonizing that I could not turn away. Rarely does a story of obsession also render in such detail the strength of character and depth of self-knowledge necessary to turn away from the object of one's obsession and face the self. This is a wise, intimate, and profoundly erotic memoir."
    – Melissa Febos, author of *Abandon Me*

"A Year of Mr. Lucky is an immersive look at dating and kink through Meg Weber's talented pen. If you want to know what it's like to be into BDSM and searching, not necessarily for 'The One,' but for something grander and even more fulfilling, read this memoir."
    – Rachel Kramer Bussel, author of *Sex and Cupcakes: A Juicy Collection of Essays* and Editor of *Best Women's Erotica of the Year* series)

"Articulate and dripping with emotion, this epistolary memoir from a Portland therapist and 'language slut' is a love letter to the city's kink scene, full of deeply insightful words on bottoming and polyamory problems, and a fitting postmortem to a compelling and all-too-brief D/s fling. If you've been romanticizing open relationships and BDSM sex, pick up this book for a dose of real talk about catching feelings, 'it's complicated' relationships, and processing need, grief, love, anger and lust."
    – Carol Queen PhD, author of *The Leather Daddy & the Femme*

"At turns radically edgy and heart-sleeve vulnerable, Meg Weber's writing will remind you what it means to be deeply human, and to be deeply yourself."
    – Ariel Gore, author of *We Were Witches*

"Meg Weber's *A Year With Mr. Lucky* is a rare offering: a memoir of erotic obsession that manages to be at once brazenly explicit and non-sensationalist. It's an interrogation of desire and torment, fantasy and transference, grief and psychodrama, self-deception and self-assertion that brings a therapist's sensibilities to bear on her own sexuality and how we negotiate the fulfillment of our needs... unapologetically transgressive and utterly poignant."
    – Elissa Wald, author of *The Secret Lives of Married Women*

"I could gush on the million, inspiring, literary feats Meg Weber has pulled off in this memoir – but I'll highlight her authorial eye. Weber never flinches but writes into the messiness of being alive, with hard won painful poignancy. She's the real deal."
    – Joshua Mohr, author of *Sirens*

www.sincyrpublishing.com
sincyr.submissions@gmail.com

Published by SinCyr Publishing, University Place, WA 98466
Copyright © 2020

A Year of Mr. Lucky Copyright © 2020 Meg Weber
Pleasing Alex Copyright © 2020 Meg Weber, reprinted in part from
*Sex and Single Girls* by Seal Press in 2000.
Wardrobe and Too Late Copyright © 2020 Meg Weber, reprinted in
part from *Wardrobe* by Rabble Lit in 2018.
Eye of the Beholder Quote Copyright © 2013 Kim Kankiewicz pulled
from fullgrownpeople.com/2013/10/09

Print ISBN: 978-1-948780-29-2

Edited by Sienna Saint-Cyr
Copy Edit by Rhiannon Rhys-Jones
Cover by Lee Moyer

In memory of my sister, Tracey.

# NOTES & ACKNOWLEDGEMENTS

A few people's names and identifying characteristics have been changed to protect their privacy. The emails between Meg and Mr. Lucky have been edited for length and clarity and are otherwise true to our actual correspondence.

Thank you to Sienna Saint-Cyr and Sincyr Publishing for believing in this book. Thank you to Mr. Lucky for allowing me to use his emails to help tell this story.

Thank you to my writing mentors along the way, especially Ariel Gore, Lidia Yuknavitch, Melissa Febos, Mary Anne Em Radmacher, and Wendy C. Ortiz. To my group from the Writing X Writers Boot Camp: Maggie, Pat, and Tanya – your feedback and support for this book kept me going and I am forever grateful. To all the writers who read bits of this in the Literary Kitchen classes, thank you for helping me shape this book and make it happen, especially Anna, Jenny, Ky, Sara Jeanne, Cecile, Jenna, Nina, Abby, Shari, and so many more.

To my amazing Women's Group thank you for being a supportive foundation through the experiences in this book, and for helping me find my voice to talk about it, not just write it all down; I miss you all. And to Erin, the incredibly talented facilitator of our Psychodrama therapy group, thank you for your support and for teaching me the skills I would need to set myself free at the end of this story.

To my dear friends August, Jenn, and Laine who read early drafts and who have been beside me through everything, I can't thank you enough.

I have had the great fortune to work with an incredible therapist off and on for more than 20 years. Gayle knows me better than nearly anyone on the planet and I am grateful beyond words for her support, tenderness, compassion, and wisdom.

A huge thank you to Heather, for everything you were to me and helped me become. Thank you especially for that moment in the late '90's at Oasis Pizza when you looked up from something I'd written and said, "You're a real writer, Meg!" Thanks for helping me believe it even way back then.

To my parents, siblings (especially Tracey), and cousins thank you for loving and believing in me.

And thank you to a not exhaustive list of others who have supported me and my writing throughout the years: Kelly, Traci, Sage, Sunny, Christine, Nicole, Chris, Greg, Kacee, Kirk, Anthony, Kylie, Cory, Sara, Molly, Sheldon, Alex, and my Writing and the Body beloved friends.

# CONTENTS

OWNING ME.................................................................................19

UNPACKING.................................................................................25

PLEASING ALEX ...........................................................................30

RIBBONS......................................................................................50

SCENE NUMBER ONE....................................................................67

EDGES.........................................................................................88

SCENE NUMBER TWO ...................................................................91

AN UNSENT EMAIL TO MR. LUCKY.................................................99

COMPELLING PERMANENCE........................................................102

DEFINE YOUR TERMS .................................................................103

COUSINS' WEEKEND...................................................................104

EMAIL........................................................................................106

LONG VIEW................................................................................108

I DON'T WANT TO WAIT...............................................................110

MISSING.....................................................................................113

PERSPECTIVE..............................................................................114

CLARITY OF DESIRE....................................................................116

THE MYTH OF FINGERPRINTS......................................................119

APOSTROPHE..............................................................................121

INTERNAL ARGUMENT ................................................................123

RADIO INPUT .............................................................................126

NOT WHAT I WANTED AT ALL, BUT ALSO NOT GIVING UP......................130

RELIEF.......................................................................................131

QUIET ON THE PAGE, NOT IN MY HEAD ........................................133

FIRESIDE CHAT...........................................................................134

WHY ISN'T THE CONFIDENT VOICE MY LOUDEST.................................139

INTEGRAL .....................................................................................141

I ACTUALLY DON'T UNDERSTAND.................................................143

LUNCH HOUR – SCENE NUMBER THREE....................................145

VOICE ...........................................................................................155

TIRED OF MYSELF .......................................................................161

TAKE THIS MEANNESS OUT OF ME.............................................162

WHILE I AM WAITING..................................................................163

SWIMMING...................................................................................166

SECOND LUNCH – SCENE NUMBER FOUR ..............................168

SETTING IT ASIDE .......................................................................176

MOVING BEYOND THE OBSESSION ............................................178

THE FIRST TIME...........................................................................182

SCENE NUMBER FIVE .................................................................184

EMOTIONAL SEDIMENT .............................................................196

THIS IS WHY I GO TO THERAPY .................................................198

RUNNING THOUGHTS .................................................................200

TRIFECTA – WEEK #96 ...............................................................201

SUGGESTION BOX ......................................................................202

TAKING RISKS.............................................................................204

FRUSTRATED...............................................................................205

HOLDING SPACE .........................................................................206

WRITING GROUP .........................................................................207

REMINDERS ................................................................................210

INTERSECTION............................................................................211

TRIFECTA - WEEK #107...............................................................213

SCENE NUMBER SIX....................................................................214

BECAUSE I'M ME..........................................................................222

CRASHING...................................................................................227

GRAVITY .....................................................................................229

MELANCHOLY ............................................................................... 231

IMPATIENT ................................................................................... 233

GRASPING ..................................................................................... 235

GRIEF COOKIES ............................................................................ 237

MISPLACED MISSING – AN EMAIL I'M NOT SENDING HIM ......... 239

CONSEQUENCES .......................................................................... 241

ONE WAY TICKET TO WHATEVER ............................................... 242

BANKING ON TOM ....................................................................... 244

STEPPING AWAY SLIGHTLY ......................................................... 246

I AM A PERSON WHO... ................................................................. 248

BLAST OFF ................................................................................... 250

THE ONE I WANTED TO SEND ..................................................... 252

BUT DIDN'T .................................................................................. 252

PREOCCUPIED AND ANXIOUS ..................................................... 253

SOME OF THE THINGS I WANT TO SAY AND PROBABLY WON'T ... 254

TRIFECTA – WEEK #101 ................................................................ 255

HOW TO NOT BE A TOTAL PUNK IN A RELATIONSHIP ............... 256

STARLIGHT ................................................................................... 257

WHAT TO DO IF YOU'VE ALREADY ACTED LIKE A PUNK ......... 258

TRUTH-TELLING ........................................................................... 265

WARDROBE ................................................................................... 267

CROCUS ........................................................................................ 270

EXPLICATE .................................................................................... 272

CALM OR TEMPEST ...................................................................... 274

CLAMORING ................................................................................. 275

VIRTUAL ....................................................................................... 277

WHAT DOES HE MEAN ................................................................. 281

TOO LATE ..................................................................................... 282

OCTOPUS ...................................................................................... 284

BACK AND FORTH ........................................................................ 286

BIRTHDAY PARTY .................................................................................. 298

ECHOES ............................................................................................... 300

TARGET................................................................................................ 302

WRITING WORKSHOP .......................................................................... 304

GROUNDING ....................................................................................... 306

CHALLENGE ......................................................................................... 307

SNARK FEST......................................................................................... 309

AN UNSENT PROPOSITION .................................................................. 312

LAG TIME ............................................................................................. 314

TEMPER TANTRUM .............................................................................. 315

RIDICULOUS......................................................................................... 317

STICK FIGURE....................................................................................... 319

WHERE I STAND NOW .......................................................................... 321

WHAT THE FUCK.................................................................................. 324

EMPTY SOLACE .................................................................................... 325

FINDING MOLLY ................................................................................... 327

SUNDAY IN THE PARK .......................................................................... 330

TIDBITS................................................................................................ 335

RELEASE .............................................................................................. 336

NOT QUITE FINISHED .......................................................................... 342

FINALE.................................................................................................. 344

ABOUT THE AUTHOR ........................................................................... 346

# OWNING ME

Owning me was written into the game, but not like this. Not a splintered heart and brittle distance. Not unmet longing. I wasn't supposed to fall in love.

I want to read a book he hasn't written yet, one that explicates the poem of us and explains how I got under his skin in ways he doesn't usually allow. His clever prose would pretend disdain for my verbose devotion but belie the truth that he loves every syllable. I want his reflections on the half-dozen scenes we did together, scenes he crafted and delivered upon me with exquisite creativity. I want to explore the intersections of our words and bodies, of power and attunement, of submission and silence.

I'm waiting for patience and for words to convey the synergy of emotions roiling within me. Sadness sings a solemn, lonely song. Anger is acutely aware of his absence. Curiosity cracks my composure when he won't communicate clearly.

His radio silence is the wrong kind of sadism. Minutes bleed into hours, hemorrhage into days, flood into weeks. I'm waiting to let go, to let what we had become just a collection of memories in the past tense. Still, the weight of waiting wears on me, again.

He is distant and guarded, but it wasn't always this way. In the beginning, oceans of words spilling from two directions tossed intrigue and interest between us. There were rules of engagement. But my heart doesn't follow rules.

The wrong part of me is owned by him. Buying it back will cost every ounce of courage I can produce. I will pay for it with every pore of worthiness I embody. I will need to remember that a broken heart is not the end of anything.

It is a beginning.


Jun 1, 2013 at 8:47 pm
Hi, I'm Meg.

The following bits from your profile caught my attention: exciting spankings, handcuffs, and your writerly love of books.

I am seeking medium-commitment fun, and like to play (but not necessarily lose at) word games. I am highly freckled and am an ethical slut. While genius seems a bit much, I definitely appreciate Tom Petty's music - esp. Into the Great Wide Open.

What does your dating or play partner dance card look like these days? Interested in meeting up for a drink and a word game and talking about what else we'd like to explore together?


*Jun 3, 2013 at 12:54pm*
*hi meg,*

*thanks for the message.*

*my dance card (and schedule in general) are alarmingly full these days, but i can usually squeeze in another word game and a chance to see if we might have compatible play interests.*

*you seem like an honest and sensible person, which is the kind i like to know. plus, freckles!*

*before meeting, i want to hear what type of kink scenes interest you most. (i've had a few dating app experiences in which everyone's time would've been saved by an early discussion of this stuff...)*

*-[redacted]*

Jun 3, 2013 at 11:34pm
Thanks for replying, [redacted].

Honest and sensible are accurate. You seem fun, quick-witted, responsible, and nefarious in delicious ways.

Nothing like jumping right into the good stuff, eh? In nearly all of my kink adventures, I've bottomed to men. Rough sex in the context of a power dynamic gets me hot. I specifically enjoy being controlled, bossed around, tied up, spanked, used sexually to please my top, verbally teased/taunted. I'm a word slut. I like to suck cock. I like having my hair pulled, and I like to be fucked, hard.

It's more about power exchange than physical pain for me. I'm not much of a masochist but I enjoy pushing my limits to please my top, especially if I get praised for it, and then I get fucked.

The intersections of pleasure, pain, power, and desire are compelling.

Does any of that match your desires, [redacted]? Will you divulge more about what type of kink scenes interest you?

Let me know if you're up for that word game and further discussion of whether we'd enjoy playing together.

*Jun 4, 2013 at 12:15pm*
*That was a pleasantly comprehensive response. Seems to me that we have numerous common interests and should certainly try out a meeting.*

*I like your willingness to answer a direct and clear request for information. I've found that to be something good subs are good at.*

*To date I've only topped women – I like all kinds of spanking, slapping, and restraint, especially in the context of general servitude. Highlights include orgasm control, breast bondage, choosing attire or lack thereof, verbal humiliation, begging... a favorite scenario is receiving cock worship while I accomplish some other task (e.g. having a drink and reading the paper).*

*I'm not a serious sadist, but I like causing some pain on occasion.*

*Let's move forward with the board game plan. How about if we tentatively set up for the evening of Friday 6/21?*

Jun 4, 2013 at 11:54pm
I agree that our interests overlap well and look forward to meeting you. The evening of 6/21 is on my calendar.

Thank you for describing what you like. Seems we could have a hell of a lot of fun together.

I generally respond well to all manner of direct and clear requests - in sub space and not.

How many women do you currently play with? Are they casual play relationships or is there a romantic/dating quality to them? Aside from overlapping interests, what do you seek in a submissive?

> *Jun 7, 2013 at 8:45am*
> *I have a primary non-monogamous partner and two other playmates. The latter are more casual than romantic, but we do dating activities (like meet for food or drink) before playing, so...*
>
> *I like creative subs who don't need constant detailed direction, and smart subs who understand how to support and enliven whatever vision I have for our activities. I like a lot of talking and begging. I don't mind a sub who suggests things, as long as it's done respectfully. Obviously, I value subservience. I don't like to punish. I get off visually, so I like a sub who displays herself well and understands that her body is always in use, even if I'm not touching her.*
>
> *What are your answers to those questions about current involvements?*

Jun 7, 2013 at 10:28pm

I have one lover who I've seen sporadically over the last seven months. It's the first non-kinky sexual relationship I've had with a man.

Creativity and cleverness are qualities I look for in a top, along with believable authority. I like clear direction but am also quite intuitive and read situations well. I like to know I've pleased my top by being praised or shown some level of appreciation. Having a ritual to open and close a scene has been useful for me. This can be subtle, but it helps me to mark the transitions in and out of scenes.

Do you use a collar on your subs? How sexual is your play? (I recognize that sex and play are subjective terms.)

Your profile mentioned you're a writer. What sort of writing do you do?

# UNPACKING

A quick glance at my phone shows no new email from [redacted]. *Guess it's time to unpack more boxes,* I tell myself. I tiptoe out of my daughter's bedroom, hopeful she's actually asleep this time. Frances, at six, isn't the best sleeper but I rely on her early bedtime for some time to myself.

It's been a month since we moved in, but my bookshelves sit empty in the cluttered living room behind four heavy boxes of books. I reach to open the top one and can barely lift it. *Good thing the boys were there on moving day.*

All five of my older brothers and both sisters helped move me out of the last house I shared with my ex and Frances. All those hands made quick work of loading and unloading furniture and boxes. My siblings didn't have a lot to say about my divorce, and there wasn't even much small talk on moving day. But they all showed up to help.

Watching my brothers carry load after load of belongings into my new apartment reminded me of helping mom carry groceries in from the station wagon when we were kids. It didn't matter whose turn it was on the Atari or what we were watching on tv. When the garage door opened and mom pulled in with a car full of groceries, every one of us dropped what we were doing to help. It wasn't a question of wanting to; it was expected, as automatic as the sit-stand-kneel routine of Catholic Mass every Sunday.

Once the truck was empty, my brothers left. They didn't even stay for moving day pizza; the work was done so they could leave. My sisters stayed longer to help me arrange furniture and make the beds – a twin in Frances's pale pink bedroom, and a queen in my orange bedroom.

I place books on the shelves in size order, knowing I'll sort them again later by genre and author. For now, I just need to empty the boxes and clear more space to walk in our small living room. Quietly, so I don't wake Frances, I flatten the boxes and carry them out to the recycling bin.

There's still no email from [redacted]. I give in and go to bed.

*Jun 10, 2013 at 2:55pm*
*that's interesting about your first non-kink relationship, rather than the usual system of moving away from a vanilla lifestyle. maybe there is no usual.*

*your bottoming style works for me - i'm a pleasant person and i like things to be cool with my sub, which includes recognition of her efforts as long as she's obedient and respectful, and acknowledges that she has given up control.*

*please give me an example of an opening/closing ritual. it seems like a practical way to define the scope of the experience. i am open to trying it. i've never used a collar, but i like them, and i can see how collaring/release is one example of a ritual.*

*while definitely recognizing that sex is a subjective term... i require the possibility of sexual activities during play.*

*i'm merely an amateur writer working on a sci-fi novel. it's fun, hard to stay on task, though! how about you?*

Jun 11, 2013 at 12:01am
I think your sense that usual means moving from vanilla toward kink is pretty common.

Your topping style will work well for me. Sexual activities are a vital part of my play; sex within the context of submission and pleasing my top is why I'm there.

Yes, I'm fond of collaring as a way to open/close a scene. My first top required me to enter his house, strip naked, and kneel until he was ready for me. As he approached, I verbalized my purpose: to serve and be used for his pleasure or entertainment. I can't recall if we had a closing ritual other than him removing my collar. I also created a private ritual of grounding to prepare myself to serve him.

Transitioning into a scene feels more important to me than transitioning out, because that tends to happen naturally as a scene runs its course if the top knows what he's doing. I also want to be clear that none of this is prescriptive or imperative.

I mostly write memoir. I've had a few pieces published - an essay about my early experiences with s/m was part of an anthology about 13 years ago. (Happy to share it if you have any interest, won't if you don't). I have rough plans for a couple of books.

Is it working for you that I ask so many questions? I don't want to be impertinent or supersede anything you might ask of me. I'll wait for a go ahead before sending more questions.

I'm enjoying this correspondence very much and am excited to meet you.

*Jun 11, 2013 at 10:41am*
*Thanks for sharing the ritual. It's hot, though more ornate than my tastes dictate. If we decide to play together, we'll have to brainstorm something simple and elegant, with a mutually satisfying verbal component.*

*On the sex-in-scenes tip: As I chat with people about their kinks I'm surprised how many folks play with an explicit no-sex (whatever sex means to them) restriction. Now I feel naive about it, but it had never occurred to me.*

*I enjoy your numerous questions - I'm interested lately in the focus of attention and answering your questions relates to that. Your questions create a pleasurable situation in which your focus is on learning about and catering to my needs and desires, which you clearly have a gift for.*

*Please send your s/m essay.*


Jun 11, 2013 at 1:37 PM
I'm confident we'll find a hot, workable solution to my desire for ritual.

I remember also being surprised in my early days of exploring BDSM how many people keep their kink play separate from sex, or rather how many people experience kink in a non-sexual way. That's definitely not how I'm wired.

I'm relieved that you find my questions enjoyable. And thank you for the compliment. I do want to discern and cater to the needs and pleasures of anyone I bottom to; it's part of the fun. Plus, this regular contact fills the gap until we meet, which helps with my sometimes troublesome lack of patience.

How many active play relationships do you like to have at once? Given that preference, how often do you play with each sub?

Is kissing part of the play you do? Where do you play - at your house? Do you play in public?

I look forward to hearing what you think of my essay, "Pleasing Alex".

# PLEASING ALEX

The *Wild Encounters* personals seemed out of my league. I was a recovering Catholic dyke from suburbia trapped behind one-way glass, peering hungrily at an unattainable world. Or so I thought. Then I found Sheldon's ad:

> No Euphemisms, NO BS. I'm a single, intelligent, honest, experienced, creative male top seeking a compatible erotically submissive woman. I like to bind, bite, spank, command, tease and much more. Limits negotiated and respected. Novice welcome. Safe, sane, and consensual.

Curiosity was the true catalyst. I thought there was magic in his language, but his words were merely colored by my ache to experiment. I craved experience under a trained hand. And I'd wanted to have sex with a man since before I came out as queer. Here, in forty words or less, was my chance at both.

Physical attraction was never the draw with Sheldon, a short, scrawny computer geek with a light brown crew cut and a crooked smile. The first time we played began with a two-hour negotiation of limits and boundaries. "This is where you pull out a menu and I pick what I want, right?" I asked, hopeful. This was all new to me; I had no clue what my limits might be.

Aside from processing the pain of BDSM, my biggest challenge was learning to communicate in explicit, precise language. Coming to terms with these aberrant desires required me to liberate my vocabulary and speak words nice girls don't use.

Sheldon was a bike with training wheels – the thrill of a new experience without any real danger. That first time we played, I stripped naked and knelt before him. When he locked his collar around my neck, a shivering thrill ran through my body. He pushed me onto my hands and knees, inspected me like a thoroughbred. Holding my breath to savor this anticipation, I was exposed, poised on the edge of a potentially terrifying experience.

At his command I sat back on my heels, hands behind my back. Every movement was calculated, each ounce of tension drawn out to its fullest. He pulled me to standing by my hair and directed me to lie face down on his bed. Sheldon was the epitome of beige and his room was proof: bare walls, off-white bed sheets, only a computer and IT books for decoration. He placed my wrists and ankles in leather cuffs with tiny padlocks. Lengths of cold, thick chain bound me to the four corners of the bed. "I decided to be nice and not freeze these first," he quipped. "Since it's your first time and all."

There was no compelling reason to fear Sheldon. His authority was a facade, not sufficient to scare me. We were merely playing with surprise and perceived threat. It was a mind-fuck. I wanted to silence my intellect and allow these new sensations to carry me somewhere my mind couldn't take me.

As he locked the final padlock, fastening the chain to eyebolts on the bed, he muttered, "Now where did I put that axe..." My mind tried to induce panic; after all, I was now chained to the bed of a near stranger, seemingly powerless. But my gut knew I was safe, which allowed me to laugh it off and play along.

The sex was fantastic. Sheldon knew precisely how to fuck me – deep, hard, and long enough to believe it might last forever. But our play was safe to a fault. He gave me a thorough introduction to BDSM but after six months I craved something faster, more dangerous.

Which brought me to Alex. Sheldon had given me Alex's name as someone who would vouch for his integrity. I regularly called her bursting with stories no one else in my life could fathom. Not only did Alex relate, as one kinky dyke to another; she had bottomed to Sheldon and understood his quirks.

Alex became the object of my obsession. She was goddess-slut-mother-whore-madam-sir-now-faster-harder-more-pain-sex-love-lust-loss. I didn't intend for it to go all those places. I never wanted to idolize her.

Before discovering kink I went through a series of friendships with women I made into larger-than-life deities, reducing myself to nothing in comparison. This also existed with Alex. It may have seemed like a match in the context of dominance and submission but playing with an actual power differential in BDSM is dangerous. Power exchange should involve people of equal influence who choose to engage this way. To feel safe in BDSM play, I need to know my own worth and willingly defer my power.

I limited myself to casual, platonic interactions with Alex. But she was a smart, sexy, literate, kinky dyke and the more I got to know her, the more my desire flared. The last chance to curb my crush was obliterated when she propositioned me at a play party. I accepted her offer, regardless of my prior resolve. Refusing her wasn't an option.

In the spoken equivalent of tripping up the stairs, I asked how to address her during this scene. "You can call me Alex," she smirked. She was confidently tender as we discussed boundaries. Next, she instructed me to remove my jeans. "Turn around," she ordered. "Let me see my canvas." As I leaned forward on my hands and knees, she pronounced me beautiful. A brilliant, shy smile crossed my face. She hadn't even touched me and I was already flying.

Alex laid me across her knee and began to spank me. Her touch was electrifying. I savored the comfort of her body beneath mine, the way our curves fit together like long-separated puzzle pieces. It wasn't the sheer physicality of being spanked that captured me but the sensual, erotic tone of her voice. Ultimately, I'm a language slut. The pain of spanking drowned in the sweetness of her words: "You're being so good." That paradox of being praised for doing something taboo was exciting.

As much as I sought physical sensation to ground me in my body, I also needed praise for how I handled pain. Sheldon never showed appreciation for how I took the pain and humiliation. This indifference stung more than any blow he dealt. Alex's adulation nourished me. Maybe it reassured me that BDSM is a viable form of sexual pleasure. Perhaps it was the mother issues that sneak their way into my relationships with older woman.

My connections with women bloom from a deeply visceral place. No one has hurt me more than the women I've loved – starting with my mother and including most of my female lovers. My attraction to men mostly manifests as emotional indifference mingled with sexual lust. Alex captivated my entire being: mind, heart, body, and soul. There was no need to invent a power differential between us. It already existed.

All too soon the spanking was over, reality interrupting like an impatient child. I slowly put my jeans back on and we made our way upstairs. Alex wanted to explore a play relationship with me but couldn't commit the required time and energy. Her solution was to conduct an e-mail correspondence in role as Dominant and submissive – she would pose questions for me to answer by a deadline of her choosing. It allowed us to engage our mutual attraction without the time commitment of an ongoing, physical relationship.

The assignments established our power dynamic and allowed her to get to know me better. Bottoming to Alex virtually elicited more genuine submission from me than anything I ever did with Sheldon.

Her blunt, direct questions demanded complete honesty. My responses dripped with candor and deference; I held nothing back, until she ordered me to write an erotic account of the sexiest scene I'd ever done.

I balked. My hottest scene was her spanking me and I wasn't willing to write that for her. Besides, behaving at every turn hadn't generated sufficient attention from Alex. Part of the allure of kink was a chance to alter my relationship to authority, to push against established limits and have them hold strong. I'd been a good girl who did what she was told; I decided to challenge her. I explained that her spanking me was the hottest scene I'd done and that I didn't want to write about it. Alex replied that *I don't want to* was unacceptable and I could choose to end the correspondence, contact her out of role to explain why I was acting out, or get over myself and complete the assignment.

Thinking I'd had my fun, I promised to write the story. She demanded an apology. Trembling with excitement, I sent an eloquent false apology; I felt no remorse for finally getting this focused attention. Then I received her summons: *Not good enough. Meet me at the Cup and Saucer 7:15 a.m. and be prepared to deliver your apology on your knees.*

As I entered the café, Alex caught my eye, then sat at a table, facing me. I perched on the chair opposite her. She glared at me, arms folded across her chest. "I'm waiting…"

I gulped, "Do you expect me to kneel?"

She nodded.

I dropped to my knees with my back to the other early morning diners. Speaking words I'd tried to rehearse, I apologized. "I'm sorry that my desire for your attention eclipsed my submission. You deserve my utmost respect and I've shown you exactly the opposite. Please forgive my rude, impetuous behavior."

My words hovered between us. I sought a hint from her steely blue eyes of what might happen next. Finally, she stroked the side of my face so gently I almost cried. "Get up," she whispered. At her touch, I was liquid. Any shame I felt about kneeling in public dissolved in the unbearable tenderness of her caress. In that moment, melting under the scorching intensity of her cool, calculated gaze, something started to make sense.

I had become an erotically submissive woman, willing to suffer humiliation in exchange for where it could take me. Subjecting myself to Alex's whim invited humiliation, but it also created an opportunity to earn her praise. As we left the café, Alex whispered in my ear, "You pleased me this morning." Blushing furiously, I thanked her.

My relationship with Alex sent me to the edges of submission. Through the lens of BDSM, I began to recognize danger and safety, pain and pleasure, submission and power, not as static polar-opposite entities, but as intricate amalgams of experience.

Pain is pain is pain doesn't always hold true. What is perceived as pain can translate into erotic pleasure in the context of submission. Submission as a powerless stance doesn't exist under the pretext of willful consent. These equations also translate to the physical realm. I offer my body to be used in ways that may be demeaning, painful, or humiliating in exchange for emotional release and sexual pleasure. It's a corporeal system of barter. As Sheldon once said, "Oh good, I get to hit you with things." It was true: he got to hit me with things, and I got to be fucked. That was the deal. But sexual gratification isn't my sole motivation for exploring BDSM. The freedom to examine my relationships with power, desire, pain, and submission far outweighs the thrill of a good fuck.

BDSM brings me home to my body in a way nothing else ever has. I consciously obliterate the boundaries of my sexuality to experience this embodiment. I dance inside the pain inflicted, feel my muscles and my spirit yield in their quest for catharsis. In exchange for this ability to feel, I willingly abdicate my power, grateful for the gift of emotional release through physical sensation.

*Tue, Jun 11, 2013 at 5:20 PM*
*I agree about regular contact – it keeps the all-important*
*curiosity alive, and hopefully the impatience at bay.*

*Aside from my partner, two or three play partners seems*
*ideal. I am super busy and don't visualize playing with*
*each more than once or twice a month, unless there is*
*opportunity for hour-long mid-day sessions. (I work close*
*to home and often go back for lunch).*

*If you mean mouth-to-mouth kissing, then no, not at first.*
*I'm not opposed but that's a high degree of intimacy. I like*
*and require kissing of my body (chest, feet, genitalia, back)*
*by my sub. I love mouths and try to use them in many*
*ways. Your thoughts on kissing?*

*My house is generally available for play. I don't play in*
*public to start with and it would be subtle in any case.*

*I'll check out your essay at home. Thanks. Also, I'd like to*
*hear what service and pleasure activities (sexual and non-)*
*you feel you perform particularly well.*


Tue, Jun 11, 2013 at 11:22 PM
Have you ever had a 24/7 play relationship? Do you switch?

Mid-day hour-long sessions could work quite well for me. That
number of partners and interval schedule seems feasible. Are you
a late-night person?

I really enjoy kissing. Although it is highly intimate, I don't shy
away from mouth-to-mouth kissing even at first. If my top puts it

off-limits, of course that's respected. Kissing other body parts is also fun for me.

Good to know that your house is generally available. I don't play in public due to the inevitability of work overlap.

What an excellent question. I perform each of these activities well: sucking cock, folding laundry, doing dishes, moderate intensity and duration foot massage or shoulder/neck massage, serving food, clearing a table/tidying up after a meal, organizing paperwork, kissing, sexy talk.

What service and pleasure activities do you particularly enjoy? (Aside from cock worship while otherwise occupied, as mentioned previously).

Do you often start with something innocuous like a board game before playing with a new sub? When we meet, are we indeed just playing word games?


*Wed, Jun 12, 2013 at 12:35 PM*
*I have not had a 24/7 play relationship and I don't switch. I feel my kink interests lend themselves well to a full-time arrangement. I've definitely day-dreamed about it, but it's not a serious pursuit. Yourself?*

*I am a late-night person. You?*

*Good to know your thoughts on kissing. Naturally, if we play, I'll decide who kisses what and when.*

*I like services like fetching objects/drinks/snacks, performance of small tasks ("reorganize this drawer"), maid-type activities (cleaning a bathroom in a revealing* outfit), *furniture play like using a sub as a table, secretarial tasks like taking dictation. Honestly, I have more interest than experience in this area, but I'm ready to explore it. I hadn't thought of folding laundry, but that's rather brilliant. More sexually-themed entertainments are physical inspections, wearing a plug while performing services, the aforementioned mouth use and body worship...*

*Tell me about physical constraints and other limits that you have.*

*I always start with something like a game - to check for craziness, make sure they have some sense of humor, and that we like each other. I don't want to play with anyone who doesn't like me.*

*Yes, just the game and some chat. After I meet someone new, I need a period of reflection before re-engaging.*

*I read and enjoyed your essay, but only once through – I want to read it again before commenting much. Poor Sheldon – I definitely looked around to make sure I had some pictures on the walls.*

*As you perhaps foresaw, these emails are getting too massive for me, given that I'm writing them at work and trying to use a lot of clarity, which takes revision. So I'm setting a limit: respond to the questions/prompts I offer and restrict yourself to one question for me per email.*

*(fyi, you sent your last email from a real email address)*

Wed, Jun 12, 2013 at 11:58 PM
I've never bottomed in a 24/7 dynamic. In the early days of my last relationship (the fourteen year one that ended last year), we were in a 24/7-ish Daddy/girl dynamic with me as the top. Then there was a tragedy in my inner circle and I wasn't able to continue in my role. It was a stretch for me even before my world fell apart from grief.

I am a late-night person. Two nights a week I'm at work or busy until 9 pm. Since I don't have my daughter those nights, they can be good times to schedule dates.

Should we choose to play together I would serve you in any of the ways you mention, at your command.

Physical constraints: Gags are challenging because I have chronic congestion from allergies, so I often breathe out of my mouth. It isn't completely impossible to use them, it's just not something I will want to do often.

Other limits:
I'm not okay with having any marks left on my body. No overt scenes in public, no obvious collar in public. I don't like rimming, giving or receiving. While humiliation in the form of name-calling (slut, whore, bitch) works for me, shaming or humiliating comments about my body are not acceptable. I'm not into piss, blood, or feces in play.

I appreciate the heads up about needing a period of reflection before re-engaging.

I can already tell you have more personality than Sheldon. I look forward to more comments when you choose to share them.

My one question has two parts: once you knew my last name, did you search the web to learn more about me & if so, what did you find that was interesting to you?

*Thu, Jun 13, 2013 at 10:36 AM*
*Thanks for the limits, that's a good, clear list that fits well with me. I don't like manufactured gags but I do like underwear in a sub's mouth. I imagine we can work something out.*

*I did a cursory search on your name once I knew it. I wanted to see your mouth, mainly. I have a logically, unsupportable belief that I can learn about someone from their mouth and the set of their lips. Then I saw your job and was intimidated. I felt that you probably have studied kink issues to a far greater depth than I have, and that I might be trite. Then I wondered if you know any of my counselor friends. Then I got paranoid and wondered if chatting with me was an experiment/case study of some kind. Then I laughed and got over it and closed the browser tab. It felt invasive (in the wrong way) anyway.*

Thu, Jun 13, 2013 at 2:35 PM
I would have been shocked if you hadn't searched for me. I'm curious what you learned by looking at my mouth. I've worked with some clients around kink issues and studied it for my own interest. I haven't experienced you as trite thus far – there's still time for that, I suppose. Chances are good that I know at least a couple of your counselor friends, particularly if they're kink or poly oriented and work in Portland – such a small town and even smaller kink/poly communities. No experiment or case study on my part – I'm in this for the action & connection for our mutual benefit. I appreciate your self-control in terms of invasiveness that didn't feel right. Thank you.

Will you please tell me about your relationship with your primary partner?

*Thu, Jun 13, 2013 at 4:19 PM*
*Other technical questions:*
*-What's your HIV and other sex diseases status? (i am free of all such)*
*-What is your position on condom use? (i always use them for anal or vaginal intercourse, and don't use them for oral)*
*-Do you swallow cum?*

*Yeah, seriously! It also happens that I'm a computer science professor, so I spend my days essentially living inside computers. I think I had the search results on my screen before I'd even considered whether I was going to check you out or not. Autopilot.*

*It's too bad you only get that one question. I'd probably make you beg for the answer anyway.*

*We've been partnered for many years and were close friends for a few more before that. We don't live together, see each other a few times a week, talk frequently, and email often. The relationship is mildly kinky. We are non-monogamous and she's my primary and I expect will remain so, meaning that I won't forge an emotional connection beyond good friendship with anyone else. We tell each other about anyone we play with.*

Fri, Jun 14, 2013 at 12:09 AM
Answers to technical questions:
- I was last tested about eight months ago, everything negative. I'm testing again this week to stay current, will share results when I have them.
- Same for me with condoms – always for anal or vaginal intercourse, not for oral.

- I have swallowed cum a few times. I am willing.

Of course you work in computer science, I didn't even need to ask. So many hot, kinky men I've met do. Autopilot indeed.

You can't blame a girl for trying for another question. I'll beg for the answer if you want me to.

I appreciate your transparency about your partnership. You touched on all the aspects of the relationship I was curious about.

What do you expect your subs to call you during play?

Please let me know when and where you'd like to meet next Friday evening.

> *Fri, Jun 14, 2013 at 3:42 PM*
> *excellent that you swallow cum.*
>
> *wait, is that just blatant flattery? if not, how do you explain a connection between tech and kink?*
>
> *no begging just yet — i need to calm things down a bit and that would not help.*
>
> *i was just listing things off as I thought of them. i'm glad it made a coherent statement about my relationship.*
>
> *i leave it to the sub to present a term that feels right, which I approve or disapprove. But i don't like 'Master', because it's silly. is using an honorific important to you?*
>
> *ah, logistics. what part of town are you in and what's your mode of transportation? i'm in southeast and ride a bike.*

Fri, Jun 14, 2013 at 11:56 PM
Part flattery, yes. You're attractive in your photos, and the way
you string words together and banter via email is sexy. And,
clearly, you've got the kink aspect covered. It's also nostalgia -
most of the men I've bottomed to work in tech.

Why do you need to calm things down?

An honorific isn't essential, but it is my preference. Something
simple, like Sir, works for me.

Please pick somewhere convenient for you. I live in N. PDX and
drive a car. I am happy to meet wherever you like.

You'll likely kick my ass at the word game. I've been playing one
with my nephew and I'm a little rusty. I assume you'll bring the
game unless you tell me otherwise.

I spent most of yesterday caring for my best friend, Summer, who
had minor surgery. I chuckled as I fetched things for her,
thinking about the list of service tasks you sent me. She offered to
write a reference to vouch for my attentiveness.

*Sat, Jun 15, 2013 at 11:22 AM*
*thanks, i feel like we both give good email.*

*the tech thing is interesting — it's opposite the societal*
*assumptions about male power and sexuality. i suspect*
*most computer science guys are tops, and i'm thinking of*
*all the high-powered CEOs who like to be fisted or*
*whatever...*

*why do I need to slow things down? we seem to have a good*
*connection and the possibility of mutual pleasure. you are*

*clearly either sane or doing a great job faking it, enough
that i'm toying with skipping a public meeting and just
hosting at my place. it makes me wonder if i'm off-balance
and should step back a bit.*

*Sir will be fine.*

*i'm curious: did you tell your friend that you had agreed to
perform similar tasks in a role of sexual servitude to a
man?*

*have you thought any more about a scene-starting ritual?*

Sat, Jun 15, 2013 at 1:04 PM
Not that there aren't crazy therapists, but I imagined that
knowing my profession might soothe any concern about my
sanity.

My weakness in this sort of situation has been that I want more
than is available. You have set clear expectations of how often I
can expect to see you. My asking those questions early on was a
proactive attempt to interrupt this issue before it starts. I would
encourage you to trust your instincts about our connection. But
that isn't up to me.

Sir it is, Sir.

Happy to accommodate in terms of location…and many other
ways, as indicated.

Yes, I tell my best friend everything.

I haven't thought about a scene-starting ritual in detail, I've been
a little distracted by the rest of our correspondence.

What kind of crazy have you encountered in subs that makes you wary?

*Sat, Jun 15, 2013 at 10:22 PM*
*I have no doubts that you are more than well-adjusted enough to be a safe companion. My concern is with violating my own protocol.*

*I understand your challenge of wanting more than is available and had sensed it, and of course read it in your essay. The hero worship comes through loud and clear and sounds like it's been a consistent source of complications.*

*Speaking of the essay, I've been re-reading it with pleasure. It reminds me how much more complex subs are than doms. The believable authority issue is interesting and made me reflect on my own abilities in that area.*

*I really liked the concept of negotiation sifting out the fear. It speaks to me about negotiation as a form of play in itself. The description of the power exchange dynamic between you and Alex is intense. And the spanking scene is super-hot – love that cooing plus spanking combo. Clever Alex!*

*It's a great document as a study and for insights into what drives kink behavior. Plus, you have an effective writing voice, which is essential – too impersonal and it's completely boring.*

*People who were not telling the truth made me wary. There was also a person who had demonstrated a high level of communication but was unable to maintain it in person and became alarmingly...coy. I don't know if she was crazy or just debilitatingly shy.*

Sat, Jun 15, 2013 at 11:07 PM
When you say the hero worship comes through loud and clear, I imagine you mean in the essay. Historically the hero worship only happens with women. I crush out on men but it's not the same. I've done considerable work on this and haven't fallen into that trap in over a decade.

I hate to use my question for this, but I'm curious how much this concerns you?

I have often thought of negotiation as a form of play in itself. I wonder about the idea that subs are more complex than Doms. If I had another question to ask, I'd inquire what you discovered in your reflections about your abilities. Maybe you'll have mercy on me and indulge an extra question.

I enjoy your comments about my dynamic with Alex. And I like knowing you thought the spanking scene was hot. Thank you for the detailed feedback and the compliment on my writing voice.

Whew! I'm relieved that neither of those kinds of crazy describe me. In person, I can be slow to warm up and therefore not as sassy as I am in writing, but once I settle in – it's on.

There is no sense in diluting the truth if I want this to work. To feel safe bottoming requires honesty and transparency on both sides of the connection.

Sun, Jun 16, 2013 at 10:40 PM
I didn't respond about the scene opening ritual last night; my
apologies for the oversight.

Perhaps something like this: Upon arriving to play, I greet you by
kneeling with my hands behind my back and state, "While I am
here, I am yours to use in any way you choose, Sir." From there
we move in whatever direction you wish. Typed out like that it
doesn't sound very elegant, but it's brief and simple. If you have
different ideas or thoughts, I'd love to hear them.

I'm not sure I agree about the comparative complexity of subs
and Doms. I think Doms have reasons that are just as convoluted
for why they play that role as subs do for bottoming. Doms also
do the complicated work to plan and orchestrate a scene, which
requires significant creativity, focus, and intention.

Based on what you know of me so far, is there something in
particular you're excited to do to me if we play?

*Sun, Jun 16, 2013 at 11:30 PM*
*The hero worship worried me slightly but not critically. I'm
not even sure how much I dislike the idea of a healthy
crush.*

*To feel safe bottoming requires honesty and transparency
on both sides of the connection. That's a damn good thesis
sentence.*

*Apology accepted. For the ritual, I think after you recite
those words, you should bend over, kiss my foot, and rest
your head there until I release you.*

*You make a good point, and I shouldn't have implied that*

*doms were simple. Topping is exhausting! I should have said: doms and subs seem to use vastly different energies in play, and the sub type is almost incomprehensible to me.*

*Yes, there is something I'm excited to do to you if we play.*

*What is the thing that you most want done to you if/when we play?*

*My idea for Friday: you come to my house and we play a word game and chat. I will have wine, but I think I remember that you don't drink. (?) I am open to transitioning into a (short) scene if we agree that it's a good thing to do. Your thoughts?*

Mon, Jun 17, 2013 at 10:31 AM
Your suggestion of my kissing your foot adds the elegance I lacked. Beautiful. Thank you, Sir.

I see you took advantage of my poorly chosen closed question. Well played, Sir. What in particular are you excited to do to me when we play?

Considering the first part of my body to respond to your question was my cunt, I'm going to say I want some part of you inside me. Fingers, cock... Of course, wanting it doesn't make it so.

This sounds like an excellent plan. You remember correctly that I don't drink alcohol. My beverage vice is diet soda — which is evil, I know, but there are worse substances one can ingest. I'll bring my own, there's no expectation for you to provide it.

The possibility of a (short) scene that night is thrilling.

Since we aren't meeting in public first, I plan to call a friend 45 minutes past my arrival to confirm that things are going well. I will also share my whereabouts with her in the interest of safety. If that's a problem, please let me know.

# RIBBONS

This date with Sir is starting to feel real, but it's still four days away. Good thing there's plenty to do around the house to keep me occupied while I wait. I'm still adjusting to time alone when Frances is at her mama's house. Half-time single parenthood is like a new pair of shoes I haven't broken in yet. My goal for this weekend is to unpack at least five boxes and start to make my new apartment feel cozy.

I haven't lived alone for almost fifteen years. Unwrapping artifacts from my life that had been boxed away signals a symbolic return to myself. One box holds photo albums from college and my high school yearbooks. From another I unpack hundreds of CDs I arrange on a folding bookshelf in alphabetical order. I'm creating a haven to soothe and ground me and help me nurture Frances through my divorce from her mama. The music of Ani Difranco and the Indigo Girls keeps me company as I unfurl into this new reality.

The white clock from IKEA looks boring on the white bathroom wall. It's the size of a large plastic dinner plate with a white background and simple black numbers that mark twelve, three, six, and nine. It needs decoration and I know just the thing. I dig through the art supply drawers in the turquoise living room to find scissors and poster putty. Now I just need the ribbons.

Framing the mirror in my bathroom are eight bows made of brightly colored, fabric ribbon ringlets with stripes or polka-dots, or contrast colored stitching. They add whimsy to the mostly plain room and they make me smile, remembering.

⚶

My sister is helping me unpack from my recent move. Which means I sort clothes to hang in the closet, and my sister lounges on my bed to supervise. "What are you doing for your birthday?" Tracey asks. It will be my first birthday post-divorce, the first one as a single person in fourteen years.

"I don't know. Probably nothing much." I haven't thought about turning 39, but it's happening in three weeks anyway.

She's quiet a minute, more focused on her phone than our conversation. "Ok, I've got it. Let's go to the beach overnight. Just you and me. The room is my treat. I've got a Groupon." Her face radiates an enthusiasm I hardly recognize.

Her generosity surprises me. We haven't gone on a trip together for years. A combination of depression, under-employment, and an eating disorder has drained much of the life from my sister these last few years. Her offer sounds too good to be true. "Let me check if I have Frances that weekend," I answer, opening the calendar on my phone. "Yes! It's not my parenting time. Let's do it!"

As I find hangers for the last few dresses in my closet, excitement buzzes in my chest. A few weeks later when I load my overnight bag into her car for our birthday getaway, I see a laundry basket full of small, brown paper lunch sacks, each decorated with a bright colorful bow of curly ribbons.

"Do you want your first present now, or later?" Tracey asks.

"Um, now I guess." Before I finish speaking, she throws one at me. I tear open the bag to find a small, red and orange striped, plastic keychain in the shape of an M. It's cute and bright and I love it. Then she shows me the one dangling from her own keychain – a W for our last name. We hit the road, singing along to James Taylor and Billy Joel on the stereo for the three-hour drive to the Central Oregon coast.

She feels like herself that weekend, like the Tracey I love and have missed. She tells me stories and asks me questions. We eat burgers and tater tots at a beach town pub. She trounces me at Nertz, the competitive, double solitaire game no one beats me at but her. We stop at the casino on the way into Lincoln City to drink diet soda around the Blackjack table. She poses me for a photo outside the casino with a handful of dollar bills fanned out to look like I won big.

On a long beach walk I push myself to tell Tracey that I'm dating a little and seeing men for the first time ever. I'm nervous to talk about it and fidget with the zipper on my hoodie as we stroll on the wet sand near the shore. No one else in my family knows that I'm dating or that what I want most is a boyfriend. It's safe to tell her. Tracey understands. She wants a boyfriend, too. She's been single most of her adult life.

I tell her about one guy I've seen a few times; he's interesting but not exactly my type. "He's too gentle, not edgy enough." Her face scrunches into disapproval as she rolls her eyes. She's skeptical of online dating and she doesn't understand my kinks. "I want someone smart, handsome, and funny," I continue. "Someone who might get along with our brothers."

Our sister and four of our five brothers are a land bridge between us in the birth order. Tracey is the second child and the oldest girl. I'm the baby, number eight of eight.

"Why would it matter if he gets along with the boys?" she challenges.

"It just does," I shove my hands in my pockets, fumble for words. "None of my girlfriends ever fit in with them, you know? I mean, I don't even fit in with them really. But I've always wanted their approval."

She nods. This isn't a new realization. "I think it's great that you're dating guys," she answers. "If it makes you happy, then it's right. You don't need the boys to approve. You've got me!"

We shop at the outlet mall one afternoon. Tracey's more fashionable than me and tells me how to dress. When a layered necklace of colorful stones catches my eye, she encourages me to try it on. "You need more color up by your face," she says, chiding me again for my stoic black and grey shirts, my everyday silver necklace and lion pendant. With her blessing, I buy the necklace and matching earrings.

Back in the hotel, we lay out all our purchases on the bed to take a photo of them. She tells a story of our grandpa, Dad's dad, who did the same thing on a trip he took once. She snaps the picture of our knickknacks and clothes to text to our cousin. At twelve years older than me, Tracey holds more family history than I do. I rely on her for these layers of family story.

Throughout the weekend, Tracey randomly tosses the small brown lunch sacks at me, each with one of those curly ribbons on it. Every bag holds a small, colorful trinket or treasure – tiny storage tins in bright pink and orange, striped paper clips, or a fridge magnet…small things that remind her of me. I love all the gifts, but my sister is the real treasure that weekend. I feel seen by her, and understood.

In the bathroom of my apartment, I glimpse myself in the mirror as I cut a three-inch strip of ribbon from each bow. My eyes show dark circles from not enough sleep, but I look content, almost happy. I carry the bits of ribbon and the clock to the table in my bright yellow kitchen. With the poster putty, I affix the ends of each ribbon curl along the edge of the clock at one of the unnumbered hours. This DIY fix for the boring clock is the craftiest non-writing thing I've done in a while and I'm proud of it. I text a photo of it to Tracey, post it to Facebook and call it a night.


*Mon, Jun 17, 2013 at 12:41 PM*
*You're welcome for adding to the ritual idea. I've*
*never had a scene-opening ritual, and I'm curious*

*what effects it will have on me.*

*I feel slight discomfort with being called Sir in email since we're not actually involved in a scene. I worry it blurs some important boundaries. On the other hand, it's titillating and probably harmless. And perhaps our dynamic is that you're slightly submissive to me even in this conversation?*

*The most exciting potential activity is verbal play – hearing how creatively you describe the ways in which you will serve as my pliant whore…preferably while in an exposed physical position where I can physically correct you if I feel you have not adequately explained yourself. I also want to bind and slap your tits, but I'm wary of leaving marks. How long does your skin retain rope impressions?*

*I generally move slow and I doubt I'll fuck your cunt the first time around, but who knows? Que sera sera.*

*Your safety plan is admirably prudent. I'll send you the address before Friday.*

*Good to hear that you'll bring your own drink. We all pick our own poison.*

Mon, Jun 17, 2013 at 11:43 PM
Thank you for naming your discomfort about being called Sir in email. I like that you find it titillating. The blurring of boundaries occurred to me, but I chose to use Sir because I do feel slightly submissive to you in this conversation. Especially once you set the one question per email limit, which I have (mostly) abided, it made the exchange seem partially conducted in role. If you prefer

that I stop, I will – not from a place of submission but out of respect for your discomfort.

In what ways do you provide aftercare for subs at the conclusion of a scene?

Hmm, you're excited to put my verbal abilities to the test...excellent. My written and speaking voices are quite divergent, with my confidence leaning in favor of writing. This has shifted significantly in many areas of my life, but I haven't tested it out in a kink setting in quite some time. It sounds like fun.

As for marks, if we play Friday, my daughter doesn't return for a few days. I have no idea how long my skin retains rope impressions, but that's plenty of time to recover.

I'm grateful for your candor about moving slowly. This helps manage my desires and expectations. Since the fucking is one of my favorite parts I'm anxious to get to that. I also know that anticipation adds to the intensity of the experience and the release.

*Tue, Jun 18, 2013 at 11:22 AM*
*Conducting this correspondence partially in role is acceptable to me. I won't worry about it since we're both cognizant of boundaries. Please continue to use 'Sir' when it feels right.*

*I have never been called upon to provide or personally needed any after-care besides verbal debriefing, relaxation, and kissing/caressing. I am open to providing whatever is needed, within reason and inclination. What's your experience with needing or providing care?*

*I can't see myself using any kind of knot or restraint that would leave an impression for a few days, certainly not during a first session. How sensitive are your breasts and nipples?*

*I've noticed that you're eager to have your cunt fucked. Anticipation is a valuable tool. Of course, telling you that you might not get fucked is designed to make you think about it more. Fun games!*

Tue, Jun 18, 2013 at 4:07 PM
Will you describe what draws you to topping and/or some of your early experiences as a top?

What you list for aftercare sounds lovely and sufficient. If a specific need emerges that exceeds this, I will communicate it respectfully. In my days of topping, more than this was rarely required.

My nipples can take quite a bit of intensity. They aren't incredibly sensitive, so a light touch doesn't register. It has been so long since my breasts have been slapped/hit/bound that I honestly don't recall how sensitive they are. It seems we're likely to find out.

I'm excited about many things we've discussed. Your toppish games aren't lost on me.

*Tue, Jun 18, 2013 at 11:45 PM*
*I'm drawn to topping because I'm contrarian and fiercely creative. I don't like to be told what to do. When people tell me to do things, I express my distaste and start planning a*

*way to do the opposite. I appreciate topping as a demonstration by my partner that they have no intention of telling me what to do, as shown by their willingness to be completely controlled by me. In my early days I showed this dominance the wrong way, i.e. without talking about it or taking care of everyone beforehand. (This can work, especially if your subby friends think you're hot, but essentially that's just rough sex.) Once I became more subtle, the requirements for finding a suitable playmate and for defining the project became more important. It reminds me of something trenchant you wrote: (i'm paraphrasing) power can only be exchanged between equals. And you can't treat equals in a shabby way or they'll just ditch you.*

*Earliest experience: in 5th grade a lovely young girl with braces who played the french horn wanted to 'go out' with me. I made her write a list of reasons why I should do so.*

*Earliest real experience: dressing up my high school girlfriend in nothing but a robe, standing her at the foot of my bed, and telling her to entertain me. Poor thing!*


Wed, Jun 19, 2013 at 11:13 AM
Your vocabulary is sexy. More than once I've had to look up a word (trenchant in this case). I find that very compelling.

I imagine it wasn't a stretch for your subby friends to find you hot. I'm intrigued that without the negotiation it was just rough sex which it seems wasn't satisfying to you. How do you describe what you get once you've added in the negotiation, caretaking, and communication between equals? In what ways is it more fulfilling for you?

Wow, 5th grade - that's early! I'm enjoying the thought of a 5th grade you making this demand of a lovely girl. The braces and french horn details are excellent.

*Thu, Jun 20, 2013 at 9:27 AM*
*Excellent that you find my vocabulary sexy and that yours is expanding. And trenchant is a good word!*

*I didn't mean to imply that rough sex wasn't satisfying, just that I didn't know what I was doing. I've since learned that I get off on communication and complicity. It's reassuring to know that everyone involved has the same interests. This was a big stumbling block for me: I've always been shocked that anyone truly wants to suck cock, for example. Incomprehensible. But many people do, and it's good to know because it takes away the sense that anyone I play with is doing me a favor.*

*To answer your question(s): Brains are the only erogenous zone. A sub who acknowledges her submission shows willingness to give up far more than just her body. I'm sure you're familiar with the process: making a girl strip and assume the doggy style position is hot... making her beg to do it first is exponentially hotter.*

*I'd ask a counter-question about your early bottoming experiences, but I feel like the essay familiarized me.*

Thu, Jun 20, 2013 at 12:16 PM
I'm amused that you find it incomprehensible that some people like sucking cock.

What are your feelings about eating pussy: do you do it & enjoy it?

Worrying that a partner is doing you a favor by engaging in the type of sex you want sounds awful. I appreciate submission in a sexual context because I can set aside my fear of whether I'm desirable to this partner or will please him sufficiently. Because that isn't up to me, it's in his hands. I thrive under the clarity and direction of a strong top. I spend a lot of my life managing situations. It's a relief to free myself from those concerns and be present in the moment and in my body through the experience of bottoming.

If there are other aspects about my kink history that you're curious about, ask away.

So much of that early exploration was about discovering what turns me on, permission to seek it out, and grounding myself in my body as a sexy, desirable woman. I didn't crave a bond with the men who topped me, I was nurturing connection with myself through them.

Reading the essay in present time I'm struck by how adamantly I claimed my sexual desire for women. Recently I've explored the ways in which my attraction to women subverted what felt like an inaccessible desire for men. Consequently, I took my already intense emotional relationships with women to this other level, in both a conscious and subconscious way, to allow myself partnership, sexual connection, and love in ways that felt safe.

The fact that this was a visible manifestation of how I have always felt like an outsider in my family was useful for me, in ways I didn't fully acknowledge or understand at the time.

I'm excited that tomorrow is Friday.

*Thu, Jun 20, 2013 at 1:16 PM*
*Eating pussy is not an act I hunger for, but when the mood strikes, I'm into it enough. How about you?*

*In almost every sexual arena I prefer to use my hands on other people and have their mouths used on me. I've never thought of it so clearly before.*

*I've heard such before, and it makes sense, especially for hyper-responsible people like I am picturing you. I've also heard subs describe restraints as a metaphor for that appreciation of bottoming – having surrendered movement and control it becomes more okay to relax into enjoyment of what's being done while not worrying about what you have to do. Again, it makes sense logically but not empathetically, for me.*

*I venture to disagree slightly with one point: it is up to you if you fail to please your top sufficiently through inattention or lack of effort...but I think that's separate from your point.*

*These might be un-compressible topics, but: Why was desire for men inaccessible? Are you actively attracted to and/or playing with women these days?*

*Sounds promising that you're excited. What's your time schedule like tomorrow? I'm free after 6pm.*

*My address is attached.*

Thu, Jun 20, 2013 at 3:00 PM

I prefer sucking cock over eating pussy. I've done plenty of cunnilingus and enjoyed it well enough. But I don't crave it.

How else are you picturing me?

I have felt precisely the way you describe about bondage. I appreciate the explicit distinction between logical understanding and your own felt experience.

Yes, your disagreement is separate from my point. I agree that how a sub performs is up to her.

Here's a brief attempt to answer why desire for men felt inaccessible…*I was told that no man would find me attractive because my family thought I was fat and not very good at being feminine. I was shamed into believing they were right. In order to be loved I had to lose weight and find a way to present myself in conventionally attractive ways. Neither of those things came easily for me. And although I got plenty of criticism for not doing it right, I didn't get any encouragement or support for learning how to do those things appropriately. So I gave up. I chose, both consciously and subconsciously, to subvert those expectations...*

It wasn't my desire for men that was inaccessible, but my being desired by men or having relationships with them.

I'm not actively attracted to or playing with women currently. The only woman I've ever played with was Alex from my essay. My primary sexual attraction is to men.

I'm available after six as well, so whatever time works for you is great with me.

*Thu, Jun 20, 2013 at 3:55 PM*
*Ha – Good question. I'm not sure how your voice will
sound, but I think you'll speak calmly and not too loudly. I
think you'll be a bit shy for a while. Physically, it seems
you are of larger-than-average size. I'm not sure how
feminine you will act, or how much effort you will expend
to be conventionally 'sexy'. I suspect you will not wear
make-up. Play-wise, I think you'll be admirably pliant and
rather well-trained.*

*Have you practiced the scene-opening ritual?*

*I understand it now about your desire for men.*

*I have questions about queer identity, but they always come
off sounding callow or bro-ish. I haven't quite got a handle
on who's using 'queer' for what, which is maybe the point.*

*Let's make it 8pm.*
*Are you allergic to cats?*


Thu, Jun 20, 2013 at 7:06 PM
It's also time sensitive, seeing as after tomorrow whatever you
pictured will be supplanted by our meeting. Those are compelling
guesses about my demeanor and presentation.

What do you find sexy in a sub - aside from compliance and
subservience?

No, Sir, I have not practiced the scene-opening ritual yet.

You are welcome to ask me whatever you want about queer
identity, bro-ish or not.

8 pm it is. Here's my phone number should you need it.

Maybe a smidge allergic to cats, but I take antihistamines that will quell any troublesome response.

*Thu, Jun 20, 2013 at 10:59 PM*
*your turn to register your predictions of my vibe...*

*i think we've been over most of this, but i like creativity and flirtatious adoration. i am not immune to conventional pleasures: outfits of revealing types, or clothes that demonstrate open access (button down shirts, skirts, etc).*

Thu, Jun 20, 2013 at 11:58 PM
I think you'll be engaging and witty in a somewhat measured, calculated way. I imagine your voice will be moderately deep and sound like you aren't from the NW - maybe a New York or Boston accent? The tone of your voice, and your delivery, will make the sexy words we've exchanged even hotter in person. Your profile says 5'11", so I guess you're tall. I think your eyes will be as expressive as your lips to indicate pleasure or displeasure. I expect your touch to be firm and confident. As a Dom I imagine you'll be clever, creative, strong, capable, and believable.

We'd been over attitudinal and temperamental aspects, but not sartorial ones. Thank you for addressing that part. Your appreciation of flirtatious adoration is good to know.

What can I expect as a next point of contact after tomorrow night?

*Fri, Jun 21, 2013 at 9:43 AM*
*Thanks for the prediction. That guy sounds smooth. It will be interesting to debrief on those.*

*Assuming neither of us is a serial killer, I think there will be a short period of silent reflection (a day? two?) and a follow-up message (from me) and then further discussion, if it's merited. Does that meet your needs?*

Fri, Jun 21, 2013 at 10:45 AM
Yes, it will be fun to debrief these perceptions. By then my butterflies will have subsided too.

Two days feels long but not unbearable. I understand that I'm not to contact you first after tonight.

I am definitely operating under the assumption that you aren't a serial killer.

See you tonight at 8.

*Fri, Jun 21, 2013 at 1:59 PM*
*Nervous, eh? About what?*

*Good. I actually don't feel strongly about this, but I do get off on giving the orders...*

*Likewise. And if you are a serial killer, it's your business, but please don't try to murder me.*

Fri, Jun 21, 2013 at 3:32 PM
Anxious & excited are more accurate, although nervous isn't totally off base. Wanting the connection and attraction I feel toward you in writing to carry through in person (excited). Wanting that to be reciprocated (anxious). Hoping it all goes well enough that this becomes the first and not the only time we meet (nervous).

Fair enough. Please don't try to murder me either. (As long as we're being explicit.)

*Fri, Jun 21, 2013 at 3:56 PM*
*That's well-put. I hope you're not trying to do any complicated work with all those butterflies!*

*My worry is that we will struggle to hit it off interpersonally (shyness? anxiety?) which could infringe on the play possibilities. I hate to miss out on fun for silly reasons.*

*Otherwise I imagine it'll all be interesting, and we'll have each met a new person.*

*also: here's my number.*

Fri, Jun 21, 2013 at 4:22 PM
If you expect nothing else of me by this point, I would think you'd anticipate articulate answers. And thank you.

Work may have been a nice distraction today, but my level of focus wouldn't have been therapeutic I'm afraid. I took the day off.

I am hopeful that struggle isn't the case with us. I genuinely like the you I've met through writing and can't quite imagine that wouldn't hold true in person.

*Fri, Jun 21, 2013 at 5:20 PM*
*To be clear, I am not seriously worried about us connecting.*

*Also, my house is a little blue bungalow halfway down the block on the north side. Park on the street.*

# SCENE NUMBER ONE
## June 21, 2013

I am driving across town to meet Sir for the first time. Sara Bareilles is singing *Brave* on repeat and I will myself to heed her lyrics and let my words not be empty. I arrive in his neighborhood too early. His street comes into view, but I drive past and turn a corner to circle the block, hoping that my memory of a gas station nearby is accurate since the orange fuel light is staring me down from the dashboard.

Anxiety swirls in my belly as I pull into the gas station. How will we fit with each other? Our words weave tantalizing stories back and forth. Will our bodies know how to do the same? Will our verbal play transfer from writing to speaking? Will our desire manifest in real life the way it does on the screen?

The radio interrupts the music streaming from my phone when I turn off the engine. Tom Petty's *Into the Great Wide Open* starts to play and I grin. We discussed this album in our first email exchange – this feels like a good omen. With the tank full I drive back to his street, willing myself to chill the fuck out. I'm still a couple minutes early.

Across from his house, I park the car and silence the music. The only sounds are my quick, nervous breaths. I gather my purse and the offering of fresh raspberries I've brought for him. A surprising calm settles in my center as I walk toward his front door. I feel sexy and strong, ready. I knock and he answers right away. My breath freezes in my throat as I realize he's even more handsome than I imagined; his pictures on his dating profile did not do him justice. He's in jeans and a t-shirt, with a warm smile in his brown eyes. Notice isn't a strong enough word for how this attraction lands in my body. As he pushes open the screen door to let me in, I step back and nearly fall off the front porch. So much for my graceful entrance.

I cross the threshold into his outstretched arms hugging me hello. "It's nice to finally lay eyes on you," I say, desperate to regain my composure. "I brought you these," I add, handing over the berries. He thanks me and begins to show me around his house. The space is warm and inviting. His style complements my own which is not going to help me keep any of this in perspective. I remind myself this is a casual play relationship. No strings attached.

He leads me through the kitchen to a room that is part art studio, part living room. One wall is lined with paintings – bold, colorful, modern art canvases. Most of the other walls hold shelves and shelves of books. There are plants and framed photographs. He's literate, artistic, sexy.

The word game beckons from a low table in the living room studio. I set my purse down and grab the soda I brought with me. He's already poured himself a glass of red wine. I perch anxiously on a chair near the table. The chair is too deep for me; if I sit back my feet won't reach the floor and I need all the grounding force I can manage right now. He notices my discomfort, goes to the kitchen for a smaller, wooden chair. "You'll be more comfortable in this." I thank him and we begin the game.

Small talk winds its way in figure eights between us. We are strangers in person but have exchanged so many words via email that intimacy already hums, connecting us. He rattles off something about house rules for the game, and I laugh, more to myself than at him. Of course this top has his own rules for the game. We take our turns, mingling conversation with the quiet, determined focus of finding the right next word to place on the board.

"Is Meg short for Margaret?"

"No, Megan." I resist telling a longer story about my name, decide instead to ask where he grew up and whether he has siblings. He confirms his Midwest roots – I knew he wouldn't sound like he was from here. He has a sister. I explain about my large family and being a Portland native.

He keeps score, his own tally quickly climbing thanks to strategic plays on double word scores, while mine grows at a much slower pace. He attempts modesty, which I find endearing. "I'm just getting all the good letters." It isn't true; he's trouncing me like we both knew he would. I'm nervous enough to just be grateful I can spell. We both smile at words with any hint of suggestion – *rope, suck, command.*

We're enjoying each other. I'm less shy than we both feared and can hold my own in our banter. I catch him off guard asking about the one overlapping connection I discovered in my brief Google search once he shared his last name. It turns out he's in a band with a friend of one of my friends, one small degree of separation that is daunting to him. I see it flash across his face as surprise and mild concern. We pick up threads of discussions we've had online, ask additional questions. With no limit here in person I revert to my over-inquisitive nature. I pause the game to step outside and call my friend, Emily, following through with my now obviously unnecessary safety plan. He will not harm me. I am not in any danger. I quickly gush that things are going well and promise to call her when I leave.

We finish the game, my score dismal compared to his. I excuse myself to the bathroom, sneak a look at my phone to re-read our scene-opening ritual. It feels likely I'll get to use those words. When I return he catches my eye and asks, "Are you game?"

My shy, giddy smile says *Fuck yeah, I'm game*...but I answer, "Yes." I move toward the kitchen chair, make eye contact again, and ask, "Should I return this to the kitchen?"

With this question the dynamic shifts. "Yes, do." The set of his gaze and tone of his voice suddenly have an edge of command they weren't infused with before. This change reverberates in my own pulse.

I replace the chair and remind myself on the short walk back that I'm allowed to want this, I am choosing to offer myself to him. I enter the room as he finishes shutting the open windows and lowers the shades. He faces me with a look of challenge and invitation in his eyes, and takes a seat on the couch. "I'll let you start us off then…"

I settle myself on my knees before him and take a slow breath, one more dose of grounding before we take off. Invoking our scene-opening ritual, my eyes locked with his, a spark of desire ignites in me. I think I see it catch fire in him too, as my words land. "While I am here, I am yours to use in any way you choose, Sir." As I bend down to kiss his foot I taste the thrill of delicious unknown adventures to come. I relax into the truth that his only expectation of me is to follow his orders.

"Stay there," he commands. He stands up, crossing the room to the bathroom. I remain still, waiting for him. He returns to the couch and tells me to resume kissing his feet. I deliver sweet, sultry kisses to each foot, taking my time. "Stop." The sound of his voice startles me. "Stand up and take your clothes off."

I rise to my feet, shy and nervous about removing my clothes. I slide my short black skirt down over my hips and let it fall to the floor. Next I pull the black and white fitted shirt up over my head. My eyes find his briefly as I reach behind me to unhook my black lace bra. I slip my arms out of the straps, let it land with my other clothing, then take off my simple black cotton panties. He looks at the pile beside me on the floor then back at me. "Fold them," he says sharply. I'm embarrassed; I should have known he wouldn't appreciate a careless heap. I pick up each item of clothing, fold them carefully into a neat stack. "That's better." His praise quiets my nerves.

"Kneel in front of me." His hands explore my body, tracing the shape of my breasts, squeezing them. "Open your mouth." When I comply he visually inspects my mouth. "Tongue out," he demands. He shoves two fingers into my mouth, and I force myself to remain still. I ignore the impulse to suck on his fingers. Not knowing what he has in mind keeps me on edge, intrigued, and more than slightly flustered. This is not an accident.

"Turn around. Lean forward on your hands and knees." He continues to explore down my back, around the curve of my hips. His silence is unnerving. I am wholly exposed, at his mercy, hopeful that this offering of my naked body pleases him.

He teases my cunt, slipping two fingers inside me. "Mmmm...." I utter, full of longing. When I press my hips back toward his fingers, he removes them. I understand the lesson instantly: That wasn't for my pleasure; it's part of his inspection.

He instructs me to sit back on my heels and wait, I watch him walk to the kitchen to fetch the bottle of wine. While he's gone, I peek at his laptop, open on the couch. On the screen are two lists: one of questions to ask me and another of things to do to me. It's nerdy, toppy, and fucking adorable.

He interrupts my moment. "I want you to refill my wine glass," he says, placing the bottle on a table next to his empty glass, just across the room from me. I start to stand up, and he corrects me. "I didn't tell you to stand."

"Yes, Sir." I shuffle to the table on my knees, facing away from him. I recall his words from our emails, how even if his hands aren't on his submissive, she's always on display for him and her body is in service to him. I hold myself with poise, hoping to appear sexy and confident. I pick up his glass in my left hand, the bottle in my right. As I tip the bottle towards the glass, nothing happens. No wine comes out. *What the fuck?* Then I notice that the cap is still on. Flushed and feeling foolish, I set the glass down, use my left hand to untwist the screw top, then pour. When I turn around to hand him the wine, he's smirking, but doesn't say a word. I feel his amusement and appreciate his restraint; I'm embarrassed enough.

He points out a basket of laundry on the floor beside him. "You'll fold this now." He sits back in his chair, picks up a book, sips his wine.

I smile. This is one of the service tasks we negotiated. I focus on my work, knowing he's watching me as he pretends to read. "How do you like your shirts folded, Sir?" I ask, holding one up to demonstrate options.

"In half first."

I fold his t-shirts and jeans, match his socks, and move on to a set of queen-sized sheets. I'm tempted to ask him for help with the fitted sheet, but decide against it. It isn't perfect, but it's folded. All the clean, folded laundry fits neatly in the basket. "I'm finished, Sir."

He sets down his book to examine my work. "Nice job, slut. You're quick at that!"

I bask in his comments. Pleasing my top through service and being praised for it sends a delicious mix of energy through me. "May I use the bathroom, please, Sir?"

"Yes, you may. Kneel in front of me when you return." Ever conscious of his eyes on me, I stride to the bathroom and back. I arrange myself at his feet and instinctively clasp my hands together behind my back. I glance at him for further instructions and notice a length of coarse black rope in his hands. "Come closer," he says. When I do, he strikes one of my breasts, then the other, with his open hand. Once my skin begins to flush, he uses the rope to bind my breasts, circling each one at the base then wrapping the rope around behind my back. When he's finished, my back is arched slightly from this bondage, which pushes my tits out. I see a tiny smile form on his lips; he's pleased with his work.

He catches me watching his expression and it changes in an instant. His face goes stern and he uses his bare hand to slap me across the face. I don't move, I hardly even breathe as he slaps me several more times. Pushing the limits of my submission, my eyes never leave his. I feel bold and aroused. "Turn around, slut," he orders.

I shift my body so I'm facing away from him, still on my knees. He gently brings my head toward his chest, lets it rest there. I am cradled between his legs, held in a tight embrace. My breath slows as I sink into this connection. He doesn't linger here. After only a minute he grabs a fistful of hair at the base of my neck and pulls it taut. He leans down, whispers in my ear, "You call yourself a word slut. I want to hear you beg to suck my cock." He pushes me off his chest, grabs my shoulders to turn me back around to face him.

"Convince me to let you be my cock whore."

My words tumble over themselves as they speed through the intersection of nervous and aroused. "Please, Sir, let me suck your cock. I want your hard cock in my mouth, I want it slick with my spit, let me suck it deep into my throat. I need your cock, Sir. I want to taste you, feel your hand at the back of my neck as you fuck my mouth. Please, Sir…"

"Well done, whore. You may unbutton my fly." I lean forward and fumble at the buttons of his jeans with eager hands. Stitching near the zipper says *Lucky You*; I nearly laugh out loud – truer words never existed. I'm exactly where I want to be, on my knees in front of him, about to serve him by giving head. It's for his pleasure, but I'm high on submission. "Is this what you want, slut?" I nod hungrily, my words already spent.

He guides me through the blow-job, directing my pace and when I'm allowed to suck or lick. Just before he comes, he instructs me not to swallow until he gives me permission. His cum explodes into my mouth. I balk at the salty liquid but do my best to hold it. He pulls out, watches me struggle for a moment. "Go ahead and swallow, slut."

I collapse into him, exhausted and exhilarated. He holds my head against his chest, strokes my hair gently and lets me hold onto him as we both come down. I feel treasured, which makes me want to cry. He gets down on the floor beside me, takes me into his arms and we lie there together, to snuggle and debrief the scene.

Eventually it's time to leave, we're both worn out. I reluctantly get myself dressed, surprised by how comfortable I've felt being naked with him. He walks me through the house to the front door and we hug goodbye. I step out into the cool night air, giddy and reeling, almost too floaty to drive. On the way home I call Emily back to report on the adventure. I tell her about his jeans that said *Lucky You* on the fly and that I've decided to call him Mr. Lucky. Once home, I collapse into bed, drunk on satiated desire.

*Sun, Jun 23, 2013 at 7:57 PM*
*I finally found a free moment to put together a response.*

*I hope you had a good night after our session. I crashed right after you left, but it was a sleep of satisfaction. Good times! I definitely smiled the next day at my nicely folded laundry and thought, good whore!*

*We should do it again. I suspect you'll concur, because you seemed well satisfied with our rapport. If not, I'm sure you'll let me know. If you're on board...mid-July looks like my next open slot.*

*The berries have been delicious with my morning granola. Thanks!*

Sun, Jun 23, 2013 at 9:03 PM
Thanks for the note. I thought you might make me wait almost the full two days just because you can. I wasn't worried, just entertained.

I'm happy that the laundry made you smile. I look forward to pleasing you in that, and many other ways, in the future. Yes, I would definitely like to play again.

I cracked myself up but held my composure when I poured your wine the other night and forgot to take the cap off. I was trying to be smooth, sexy, and confident. That didn't help. Did you catch that? Were you entertained?

*Tue, Jun 25, 2013 at 9:14 AM*
*good to hear that you want to play again. i'll rev up the old top-idea generator and find a long rope. you will look around online, find a collar you'd like to wear, and send me a link to it for my consideration.*

*july 17th is most promising day. can we hold that one open for later confirmation?*

*that's two questions! but yes. i definitely stifled a chuckle. i was going to say something snide, but then i thought eh, she doesn't drink wine, so it's an understandable mistake...*

*fyi: my communications will be more spaced out for the foreseeable future. not much time for email right now.*

Tue, Jun 25, 2013 at 12:51 PM
Excellent. Have fun with that top-idea generator. In the meantime, I promise to enjoy imagining things you might do to me.

July 17th is held for you.

Why yes, it is two questions. I'm confident you realize how challenging that limit is for me.

I wish I had seen you stifling the chuckle. Snide would have been okay. I think I expected it had a cork and you had left it out. I was quite focused on being on display for you.

I'll miss the regular email contact, but I understand. I've been writing about the other night, which keeps me engaged. Are occasional, brief emails from me with no expectation of a quick response acceptable?

Here are links to two different collars I like, Sir. The first is my favorite, but if you prefer a locking one the other is a close second. 19 inches.

> *Wed, Jun 26, 2013 at 8:51 AM*
> *enjoy your imagining. your collar choices are noted.*
>
> *challenge is good. and i was kidding: i don't consider that two questions.*
>
> *ah, it was the screw-top that got you! there's a pun in there somewhere… i liked seeing how you handled it and if you were embarrassed.*
>
> *you've been writing for your case study? kidding. do you blog your writings?*
>
> *certainly, brief emails are acceptable. i'll let you know if they stress me out or something…*

Wed, Jun 26, 2013 at 8:15 PM
Good to know not all my compound questions count as pushing the limits.

I was embarrassed; I imagine I blushed mightily. What else did I handle in a way that you enjoyed?

Right, my case-study. In the interest of diligent research, I hope you will respond to the attached survey when your busy schedule permits.

No, I don't blog those writings. They can be made available if you are interested.

Yes, Sir, please advise if my emails become problematic. I respect your time and the clarity about your availability. I don't want to overstep.

*Thu, Jun 27, 2013 at 10:42 AM*
*You did well in breast bondage... you noticeably arched your back more, improved your posture, and stuck your tits out. Perhaps it was the ropes though.*

*Hilarious. I assume the NSA is reading this email right now.*

*I'm wary, but sure, send along your writing if you're comfortable with it.*

*Sub performance rating - session 6/21*
*A brief survey for self-rating and rating by Sir of my performance in scene.*
*Mr. Lucky's response:*

*Delivery of scene-opening ritual*
*Needs work 1 to 7 Well done, slut! = 5*

*Responsiveness - verbal (including appropriate use of Sir)*
*Speak up, bitch! 1 to 7 Good job, whore. = 3*

*Responsiveness - bodily*
*Am I having any effect on you? 1 to 7 I can tell you're mine by the way your body responds to me. = 4*

*Begging - word choice, level of urgency, believability, stamina*
*I thought you were a word slut?! 1 to 7 Good whore, you convinced me you wanted it. = 5*

*Attention to presentation*
*Sloppy, whore, I hope you can do better than that. 1 to 7 Well done, slut. I enjoyed watching you. = 4*

*Pain/sensation handling*
*I need you to take more, bitch. 1 to 7 You took it well, slut. = 5*

*Service tasks performed: cock-sucking*
*You claim to be a cock-whore and that's the best you've got? 1 to 7 Good work, slut. You'll likely get to swallow my cum again. = 2*

*Overall satisfaction with scene:*
*Slightly better than bad t.v. 1 to 7 Thoroughly satisfying, eager to do it again. = 4*

*Any other feedback you'd like to share in your own words?*
*the slut gets bonus points for quick response to commands and excellent clothes-folding skills*

Thu, Jun 27, 2013 at 11:55 AM
Thank you for the feedback. The rope was sexy.

I'm relieved that you found it hilarious. It was either going to land well or annoy you.

Why are you wary about reading my writing?

Thank you for taking the time out of your busy schedule to respond to the survey. The data is much appreciated as is your unexpectedly quick reply.

It is helpful to know which areas need improvement. I feel embarrassed to have scored so low in cock-sucking. (Your reply might be a mind-fuck, but it's also possible that I was just that bad at it.) It goes to show that eagerness and desire do not equal knack. I hope you'll allow me further opportunities to master this skill, Sir. I very much want to excel at this for your pleasure.

*Thu, Jun 27, 2013 at 6:35 PM*
*Now, if you send a survey every time we play it will rapidly become annoying. Are you sharing your self-evaluations?*

*I'm wary out of habit. And I'm worried about imbalance in our levels of engagement. I need our scene to be an occasional/monthly facet of my life, and I would be uncomfortable if it's a much bigger part of yours. Clarity: I am not saying that I think this is the case currently.*

*No, you weren't bad at cock-sucking – but I have precise ideas of the correct performance of this service, and there's a lot of possible improvement left.*

Thu, Jun 27, 2013 at 11:21 PM
I have no intention of repeating the survey, it was fun and served a purpose once.

(This part gets wordy - sorry. I whittled it down as neat as I could, but had more to say than I thought.)

Your candor and clarity are appreciated. We both know this type of imbalance can be the downfall of a compelling connection. I won't allow that to happen between us. Presently there is extra energy for me here because: I enjoy our email interactions and the ways we both show up here; I liked playing the word game and chatting with you; the aesthetics of your space resonated with me way more than I expected (and good lord your home has so much more character and personality than Sheldon's ever dreamed of!); the scene was hot and felt incredible; I'm a little bit giddy about playing again and being instructed to pick out a collar. I am integrating all of this and letting it settle in. The extra energy will dissipate as it becomes part of me.

Your playing along with the survey and sharing how our connection fits into your life contributes to this process. Those are pieces I needed your help with.

Offering to make my writing available to you came more from a place of submission (i.e., my process about scening with you also partly belongs to you) than of wanting you to read it. I didn't make that clear initially.

It's mostly snippets of moments that have stayed with me from our play. Writing allows me to return to them repeatedly to savor or learn from or just feel into again. There are also many questions I won't likely get to ask you; it helps me process them even if they aren't asked and answered.

Your feedback and clarification about cock-sucking is reassuring and helpful. Thank you.

Tangential follow-up: all my STI screenings came back clear.

Sub performance rating - session 6/21
A brief survey for self-rating and rating by Sir of my performance
in scene. Each question has a scale of 1-7.

Delivery of scene-opening ritual = 4
Responsiveness – verbal (including appropriate use of Sir) = 3
Responsiveness – bodily = 5
Begging, word choice, level of urgency, believability, stamina = 4
Attention to presentation = 5
Pain/sensation handling = 6
Service tasks performed: cock-sucking = 3
Overall satisfaction with scene: = 6
Any other feedback you'd like to share in your own words?
Sir was creative and sexy. His presence was commanding and his
authority believable. I liked the feel of his hands, and his eyes, on
me.

Fri, Jun 28, 2013 at 11:14 AM
If I had whittled more (or taken an axe to it) it would boil down
to this: I am enjoying a healthy little crush on you. I'm not
worried about it overflowing. I don't want you to worry about it
either.

I'm afraid all the other words I wrote might come across as
defensive and that wasn't my intent.

*Fri, Jun 28, 2013 at 2:47 PM*
*Excellent. I'm glad to hear all that, I understand the*
*situation, and I like how you said it. I think we're on firm*
*ground.*

*I suspected that was the spirit in which you offered your*

*other writings. I thought of incorporating it explicitly:*
*bring your writing to our next session and I'll read it while*
*you <insert humiliating task>. But I actually don't like*
*everything about that idea, so it's a no go.*

*Congrats on the test results, and thanks for letting me*
*know.*


Fri, Jun 28, 2013 at 4:25 PM
I am grateful for your understanding and that you liked how I
said it (and told me so). The brevity I sought was elusive. I agree
that we're on firm ground.

Of course you suspected that about my writing, because you are
aware, attentive, and attuned. I don't like everything about that
idea either, so I'm relieved you decided against it.


*Mon, Jul 1, 2013 at 11:59 AM*
*That's the central challenge of email communication:*
*brevity vs. clarity...*

*Anyway, the ground is firm.*


Mon, Jul 1, 2013 at 10:08 PM
Another difficulty with email is the lack of sensual details –
inflection, tone of voice, getting to see a smirk or smile instead of
imagining it. But yes, brevity vs. clarity is an inherent struggle
here. Good thing we both like words quite a bit.

Each time either of us uses the word firm I think about your firm
hands on my body, slapping my face (that was my first time being

slapped in the face btw), spanking me, your grip in my hair. It's an arousing, persistent tangent.

Please tell me about your fascination with mouths: why they're compelling to you; what you believe you can tell about a person by looking at their mouth; why you prefer others to use their mouths on you and to use your hands on them. If you're being a stickler, you can answer just one part of that, but I'm curious about all of it.

When I spilled a bit of your wine that night, I almost licked it up instead of using a tissue. I think you might have enjoyed watching that.

> *Thu, Jul 4, 2013 at 10:09 PM*
> *yeah – i definitely don't understand people who communicate by text message. it's like email without any hope of nuance...*
>
> *my firm hands on your body is the right thing to keep in mind. i think of it as manhandling which is maybe more gendered than it should be. how was the face slapping? too hard? too infrequent? i enjoyed it, especially doing it for no real reason besides pleasure.*
>
> *i'm being a stickler: mouths are compelling b/c they're so intimate! and because they are so important. food, speech, oxygen, and carbon dioxide all depend on the mouth more or less.*
>
> *any time i have a sub kneeling on her heels, head tilted back and mouth open waiting for whatever i want to do with it or put in it, visibly abdicating power over the many*

*important functions of the mouth so that i can enjoy it...whew.*

*also, fucking a cunt is nice because of friction. fucking a mouth is better because friction+suction+tongue friction plus the aforementioned issues...*

*indeed, i would have enjoyed watching you lick up spilled wine and not least b/c you don't drink.*

*i went by Cup and Saucer a few times today and thought of your essay.*

Fri, Jul 5, 2013 at 12:02 AM
I appreciate the immediacy of texting but abhor the lack of depth.

I can't think of a synonym to manhandling that conveys the same sense of physical intensity and ownership. The face slapping was hot. It's something I've often fantasized about and was eager to experience. It was not too hard. For a first time the frequency was effective. More would be welcome in the future especially since you enjoy it.

Mouths control multiple functions through one access point and make a sub extra vulnerable, all for your own pleasure. No wonder they're intoxicating for you.

Mmm...yes. Just reading that makes me want your cock in my mouth. Plus, I have so much improvement to make in this area.

Yes, I thought the fact that I don't drink would be especially compelling. Next time I'll follow my instincts more.

It's fun to know my essay crossed your mind today.

*Fri, Jul 5, 2013 at 3:17 PM*
*your reaction to the face-slapping is noted.*

*vulnerability is a big part. this is also why i had your tongue out when you showed me your mouth. the tongue is the last line of defense. once you surrender that you are like a vessel that i can fill however i wish.*

*thanks for reminding me that i need to think about a cock-sucking training regimen...*

*it's an interesting point – you doing something you would not normally choose to do is transgressive and erotically valuable. Is it because in cleaning up wine that way you are essentially acting not as yourself but as a dish-cloth? or is it that i like thinking that you would drink half a bottle of vodka for my amusement, if i told you to? [not that i would do that - too abusive]*

*so far so good for the 17th. i'll let you know about time.*

Fri, Jul 5, 2013 at 11:36 PM
I enjoy when you explain the reasons for your actions. I can often intuit your motivation but not always.

You're welcome for the reminder. You've got me curious about what such a regimen will entail.

Good phrase, erotically valuable...yes, this is the essence of submission: ceding control to my top in order to please him and challenging my own limits in service to him.

Partly it's both - becoming an object in that way, offering myself or being used as a dish-cloth by you, but also you undoubtedly get off on the idea that I would abdicate so much control in the service of your desire.

Do we get to play games again sometime?

> *Mon, Jul 8, 2013 at 3:34 PM*
> *I'm curious what it will entail, too! no experience in this area.*
>
> *it's a heady mix. and i think your latter point is well-put. there's also an attraction in you doing it without consulting me, in an effort to please me, which makes you vulnerable to my displeasure.*
>
> *sure, we can play games again. i think it's best if we do it before a scene. i tend to want to be alone after playing – not immediately after, but shortly.*

Mon, Jul 8, 2013 at 10:42 PM
I have faith in your creativity, Sir. And I appreciate your transparency.

It's thrilling that you called out the vulnerability. Even telling you I considered licking up the wine invited the possibility that the idea would displease you. That's a risk of following one's instincts as a sub. And it's ripe for mind-fuck too, which keeps a sub on edge. It is intense and compelling.

As a sub, there are many opportunities to decide whether to act on my own or to consult my top first. I tend toward asking permission. I did quite a bit of that in our first scene, to the point that I wondered if it was too much.

What can you tell me about your desire to be alone after playing?

*Wed, Jul 10, 2013 at 12:07 AM*
*No point faking it. And it's fun to think about training your mouth. Perhaps you will be required to submit an idea.*

*Intense and compelling, yes. Pretty god damn hot, frankly.*

*Seems hard to go wrong asking permission though, as long as you have a respectful attitude.*

*I process alone, I guess.*

Wed, Jul 10, 2013 at 12:34 AM
My idea is lots of opportunity to practice on you.

What does your post-scene processing entail – or, phrased differently, where does scening take you?

# EDGES

I'm terrified that our connection is tenuous and he's on the edge of disengaging. What if I'm too much or not enough? What if I mess it all up?

It's been two days since I wrote him last. This impatience is so like me. Playing that night confirmed that I want him. Waiting a few weeks to play with him again just stokes my desire. And now I'm waiting longer for responses, too. Sometimes I don't even notice that I'm holding my breath as I check my email, until I release an exaggerated sigh when there's nothing from him.

The email I've drafted (but won't let myself send) asks if my sassy mouth got me into trouble again. I almost wish it did – that sort of trouble can be fun, and it means I might get more attention. Writing things I'm not sending to him helps me manage the extra tension of waiting, allows me to process some of this on my own without relying on input from him.

This dynamic is edgy for me. We play at appropriate behavior: respect for boundaries, submission to his will, being whatever he expects of me. And we toy with punishment – he orders me to write an apology for my written indiscretion, when I dared to shift the focus away from him onto myself. We're playing at it but that edge is lucid for me, the fear that I really did do something wrong, not as part of the sexy dynamic we're creating, but in an end game way that might make him not want to risk playing with me. When I don't hear from him for a couple of days, my thoughts revert to the fear that I fucked it up, that I wrote something wrong, said too much or not enough (often in the same correspondence).

Tangible evidence from his emails points toward him enjoying this connection. I want to trust that. I want it to soothe me. I need to hold onto myself when I'm afraid, to breathe through it and not have the only resolution be an email from him. I need other voices as sounding boards of support. Or I need to actually listen to the ones I have.

*Fri, Jul 12, 2013 at 10:35 PM*
*your question about my post-scene process is a good one because I have no idea what the answer is...*

*post-scene processing:*
*part of it is that it's my social nature to spend energy making sure everyone is having a good time, so i can't focus on myself if i'm not alone. part of it is dedicated hedonism and figuring out what I liked and why.*

*part of it (and i suspect this is typical in men) is that i experience a radical drop in my sexual drive after i cum. i usually want to stop playing and get back to fixing the house or paying bills or whatever is on the to-do list. the post-processing alone time is for managing that transition.*

Sat, Jul 13, 2013 at 12:48 AM
Having only interacted with you one on one it's interesting to consider your social nature. Dedicated hedonism has a nice ring to it.

Is it challenging for you to stay present in the post-scene debriefing time with a sub? (I experienced you as present after we played, for the record. Tired, but present.)

Maintaining eye contact with you during the scene opening ritual was intense in a positive way. It almost felt inappropriate—a sub ought to avert her gaze—but also felt essential. That might not have been the case for you.

> *Tue, Jul 16, 2013 at 6:28 PM*
> *hmm, lots to answer and i have no time! perhaps later.*
>
> *8:30 pm tomorrow.*
>
> *clothing: pants and a shirt that can be pulled down to expose your breasts without suffering damage.*

# SCENE NUMBER TWO
### July 17, 2013

*He wants me enough to play again.* This is my mantra as I drive to Mr. Lucky's house for our second scene. I'm dressed, as instructed, in a pair of jeans and a hot pink t-shirt with an elastic neckline that lends itself to being stretched. I hope it's sexy enough for him. At the very least it meets his requirements.

I arrive a few minutes early and park across from his house. I sit in the silent car and make myself take several slow, deep breaths. I'm nervous and anxious. *Will he kiss me tonight? Will he fuck me?*

He opens the door when I knock and invites me in. "How are you?" he asks, pulling me into a hug.

"I'm good. You?"

"I'm good, too. Is there anything I need to know before we start?"

"Not that I can think of."

"Great. We'll play in this front room tonight," he says. "Take your shoes off, then come into the center of the rug to start the ritual."

I step out of my black flats and set them by the door. There's music playing on the turntable, some sort of jazz. He's on the love seat waiting for me. I kneel before him, find his eyes, and recite my scripted line. "While I am here, I am yours to use in any way you choose, Sir." I bend forward to kiss his bare foot and wait there.

"Sit up," he commands. When I do, he reaches behind me to unhook my bra, slips each arm out of the strap, and pulls the bra out from under my shirt. He pulls the front of my shirt down beneath my breasts, leaves them to hang loose. He slaps one, then the other, alternating. The impact surprises me, but I like it.

"I'm going to work that mouth of yours tonight, train you to suck my cock precisely the way I wish."

"Yes, Sir," I answer around a beaming grin.

"But first you'll turn around, unbutton your pants, rest your head on the ground and present your ass to me with your legs spread."

I turn my body away from him, undo my jeans and slide them and my panties down past my ass. He doesn't make a move. He seems to be testing my patience just because he can. I rest there, on display for him.

He leans forward and slides something soft, smooth, and cold beneath my right ankle. I hear him fasten a metal buckle then reach to attach a matching cuff to my left ankle. He walks in front of me and pulls me up to my knees by my hair. In his hand is a beautiful red glass phallus, flared at one end. He hands it to me with this instruction: "Insert this in your ass while I watch."

I instantly flush and begin to panic but try to maintain my composure. *What if I can't reach to put it in? What if I'm not graceful enough?* He takes his seat behind me again, ready for me to show off for him. *There's not even any lube! I spit on the end of the plug to approximate lube, hoping that helps.* I lean forward to balance on my left arm and reach behind me with my right hand. The tip of the plug points toward my asshole. It takes a minute to shift my body enough to reach around my wide hips and butt. I am stubborn and determined to complete this task for him. I push the smooth glass as far inside me as I can, blushing furiously from embarrassment and effort.

"Good work, slut." Now turn around and face me, on your knees still, hands behind your back.

As I turn around, the plug begins to fall out. I reach back to fix it and manage to get it in again. But within a minute it slips out again. I read disappointment on his face when I look at him.

"That's too bad, whore. Now your ass won't be ready for me to fuck later."

In my rush to reassure him I blurt, "It will still be ready, Sir."

He slaps me across the face, hard. "There will be no contradicting me."

"Yes, Sir," I acquiesce. If I'd had more footing, I might have argued the point, but my job was submissive service.

"I have other uses for your mouth, slut. I'm going to show you a series of exercises to loosen up your jaw. And while you do them, you'll answer any question I ask of you." He walks me through various stretches, instructs me to open my mouth as wide as possible, then shift my lower jaw side to side. I'm not allowed to close my mouth to speak.

"What's a whore like you appreciate about cock sucking?"

"Service, Sir. Being used."

"Do you like the taste of cum?"

"Not really, Sir. I swallow to please my top. It isn't about taste, it's about power."

"Damn right it is," he agrees.

I know I look ridiculous moving my mouth in every direction this way. It's humiliating. And he's enjoying every minute of watching me squirm and struggle with it.

Just when I think his questioning will never end, he allows me to close my mouth. My jaw is tired, and I appreciate the break, however brief. He pulls his cock out of his pants and I whimper. This is what I've been practicing for, after all.

"Are you ready to suck my cock, slut? Is that what you want?"

"Yes, Sir," I answer. It takes all my submissive self-control to wait for permission.

With his hand at the back of my neck, he guides his erect cock into my wide-open mouth. "Suck," he commands. I use my tongue and the roof of my mouth to create suction, careful to avoid any contact with my teeth against him. "Can you take it deeper?" he asks. I try to nod, but he interrupts me. "Answer me when I speak to you," he insists.

"Es, thir," I mumble.

He controls the pace with verbal instructions and by physically moving my head when necessary. I relax into his clear, patient direction. After several minutes, he pulls me off his cock, tells me to rest my head on his knee. I look up at him, grateful. He shushes me, tells me just to rest. "You did well, slut. Now there are chores to do while I read the paper."

He points to the vacuum cleaner and instructs me to clean the floors of this front room, adjoining dining room, and the small bedroom. "Start in the bedroom," he orders. I stand up and get to work. Everywhere I go, the clips attached to each ankle cuff drag on the floor. They announce my every move. This, along with my tits hanging out of my shirt, makes me feel exposed, which I know is the point. I unplug the vacuum when I'm done and coil up the cord before walking back to kneel before him for my next instructions.

I see that he's laid out a futon mattress on the bedroom floor I vacuumed. Some rope and two condoms rest on the mattress. He only uses condoms for fucking. I'm thrilled. He used his hands on me the first time, but hasn't yet fucked me with his cock and I want it. I'm hungry to feel him inside me.

"You're certain you're finished?" he asks with barely a glance at me. He casts his gaze across the room to the dining room table. I follow his eyes and see what he means - I didn't push the chairs back in around the table. Embarrassed by my oversight, I quickly walk back, set them in place, and return, dropping to my knees in front of him with my hands behind my back.

On a table near the end of the couch is a collar, the one with smooth red leather on the inside and black leather on the outside, the one I picked out online at his instruction and hoped to earn the chance to wear by pleasing him. He watches me notice it. As if in response, he outlines what will happen next.

"First you'll fold my laundry. Then you'll beg me to fuck your ass. I'm going to fuck you, and then you'll thank me for it. If that all happens in a way that pleases me, you'll get the chance to wear the collar you picked out."

My body responds to his words; a cascade of heat rises in my cheeks; my cunt gets wet at the thought of begging to be used by him.

Folding his laundry is fun for me. I love his t-shirts with obscure band names and pop culture references. When all the clothes are folded, I stack them in the laundry basket. "I'm done with your laundry, Sir."

He looks up from the newspaper. "That was fast. Go into the bedroom, remove the rest of your clothing, and lay face down on the mattress." I stand up and rush to follow his order.

He enters the room, binds my hands together above my head with a length of rope, and sets something cold, smooth, and lightweight on the center of my back. I can't figure out what it is. After a moment he removes it from my back. I don't pay much attention because I'm preparing to convince him to fuck me.

"Time to beg, slut. Make it good."

"Please, Sir. Fuck my ass. I want to be your anal whore. Use me, Sir. Pound your hard cock into me. Please, Sir." My begging must be sufficient because with a bit of lube and not much further prep, I feel his cock nudge at the edge of my ass. He pushes into me slowly and I breathe into the pressure. I stretch around his cock and lose myself in the fucking.

When he's finished, he pulls his cock out of me and goes to the bathroom to remove the condom and wash his hands. Only when he returns to untie my hands do I discover it was his laptop on my back. I turn my head and see it still streaming the porn he watched as he used me. Surprise knocks the wind out of me. *Why does he need porn when*

*I'm here in the flesh to be used by him?* I feel shame and wonder if I'm not really sexy enough to turn him on. Or maybe it's a Top thing.

"You may use the bathroom, if you wish. Then meet me in the front room, on your knees in front of the couch." He walks out of the room. I slowly get up and do as I'm told.

Back in the living room, I kneel before him. He's holding the collar in one hand. "Would you like to wear your collar, slut? You've earned it." I force myself to keep my gaze lowered, but I'm beaming.

"Yes, please, Sir."

"Lean your head down," he says. When I do, he fastens the collar around my neck. It fits just right. "I bought myself a matching leash, they make a nice set," he tells me.

"Good idea, Sir." Leashes aren't my thing, but I'm beside myself with his collar on me.

"Lie on your back and use your hand to get yourself off." His offer shocks me, I don't expect permission to orgasm. I lay myself down and use my right hand to work my clit, willing myself to come. I'm turned on from being fucked and from wearing his collar. But I'm distracted and can't get off.

"Do you need some help, slut?" Before I can answer his fingers are in my cunt. I gasp and figure this will push me over the edge. I thrust against his hand, moaning and writhing on the floor. I'm so close. I'm louder now, mostly from frustration. He abruptly stops fucking me, and I realize he thinks I came. I didn't, but I'm exhausted and ready to stop.

I sit up and lay my head on his lap. He strokes my hair and we rest there together for several minutes before he reaches to remove my collar. "Thank you, Sir." I manage to say.

"You're welcome, slut," he answers.

We reflect on the scene as I find my clothes and get dressed. I struggle for words to ask about the porn. "No, it's not that you're not sexy enough. It's part of objectifying you in the role. Like the videos, you're just another thing to use for my pleasure." I tell him this makes sense to me, and it does. Being objectified is hot for me. But I can't shake the sense that he needs this added content to get off with me.

On the drive home, I realize his mouth has never touched any part of my body. Tonight I wanted him to kiss me. He is tender with me in other ways, but he won't use his mouth on me.

*Fri, Jul 19, 2013 at 9:31 PM*
*I had fun on Wednesday. Kudos.*

*Yup. It takes an effort to stay present post-scene, which I don't begrudge. The eye-contact is intense. I don't think it's inappropriate given the subsequent action.*

Fri, Jul 19, 2013 at 11:47 PM
Thanks for writing back.

I had fun too. Credit goes largely to you for planning and executing a lively, varied, sexy as hell scene.

What stands out for you about our scene the other night?

I enjoy how we both experience the scene-opening ritual as potent. Yay us for constructing something that works so well!

In our post-scene debrief, we talked about more upcoming interactions: something social; a weekday lunch hour scene; and a longer scene roughly a month out. Please let me know if you'd like to take the initial stab at scheduling any of that. I recognize this next month is probably challenging schedule-wise for you.

*Tue, Jul 23, 2013 at 12:16 PM*
*i'm dashing this off on lunch break, so it might be full of*

*grammar errors, etc...*

*a combination of changes at work and home have totally disrupted my internet communication habits. i am working on building new systems that will allow me to respond more often.*

*thanks for recognizing that scheduling is challenging! right now i'm on overload and can't plan anything. i'd like to pause for a few weeks until i get my act back together. does that work for you?*

# AN UNSENT EMAIL TO MR. LUCKY

I told myself before your email came in that whenever it arrived, I wouldn't respond for at least 24 hours. This is not for my benefit, at least not directly, but for yours. I know you're overloaded. Generally, when I get an email from you I do a little happy dance - sometimes literally, most often figuratively. I rejoice at another thread in the connection we're weaving. And then I write you back at my earliest convenience. Sometimes my response is back in your inbox within ten minutes of reading your message. My words burn a hole in me as surely as spending money in my pocket.

Learning that you don't make me wait as part of some toppish whim, helps me unearth some ability to trust our connection. I am certain that we have fun together. The scenes we've done have been hot, creative, and satisfying. We both enjoy email when we have the time to fully participate.

So now you want to pause for a few weeks and you want to know if that works for me. What, really, is my option here? What I want is more connection with you in a variety of contexts. Given that, my only choice is to say *of course, take the time you need.* But can I do that, honestly, without expecting that my graciousness now will be paid back with increased availability when your partner leaves?

You already know I want more. Being a catalyst for additional stress in your life could reduce the likelihood of growing our connection. I genuinely care about you; I don't want you to be stressed out, for your own sake, for the quality of your life right now, not as some investment that I hope yields a generous return for my benefit.

So does it work for me? Sort of.

Part of me is confident that this is about the busyness of your life and not about us. Part of me wants to find a middle ground - maybe schedule something for a month out. Both times we've played we reserved the time three weeks in advance. So if we pause for three weeks, and then it takes three weeks to schedule something - that's six weeks away. Six weeks out is early September - when my daughter goes back to school and around the time your partner leaves. All sorts of things will shift then.

OK, Meg, so what if it does become six weeks before you get to see each other again. Can you deal? Is it worth the wait?

Part of what I'm digesting is the contrast between people you play with and people you date. I'm not clear how you differentiate between them, but I feel definitively placed in the category of play partner, without any possibility of dating you. This could be a misperception. I don't have enough information about you to discern whether I am happy with my lot. Don't get me wrong - I adore bottoming to you. The attention you offer in our scenes, and in our emails when you're present in them is intense and appreciated. But I'd like to do other things with you too, friendly, date-like things like play board games, talk on the phone occasionally, share meals together. Basically, I either want to date you, or be good friends in regular contact who also play out sexy scenes together.

Reviewing your email just now, I wonder what exactly pause means. Does it mean no contact whatsoever? That would be really challenging for me. Does it mean not planning anything but continuing to email in the meantime? Do you not know what it means either?

Wed, Jul 24, 2013 at 5:26 PM
That's a lot of change all at once. Good luck sorting it out.

I appreciate your clear, direct communication about this. Thank you. Yes, it works for me. It isn't my favorite option, but I don't in the slightest begrudge you the necessary time to acclimate to all the recent shifts in your life. I want that for you. And...the connection we have is worth waiting for.

Here's hoping you find moments of rest, relaxation, joy, and productive creativity in the midst of all the overload.

# COMPELLING PERMANENCE

It's difficult for me to hold on to how compelling I am – as a person, as a woman, as a lover, as someone to be in relationship with – when that is not actively affirmed by the object of my desire. When I'm with Mr. Lucky and he interacts with me as the sexy, intelligent, funny woman I am, it feels incredible. What doesn't feel amazing is the idea that all of that is diminished when I'm not the focus of his attention, particularly because I don't get to be front and center in his frame all that often. He has a primary partner, a very busy work life, other social commitments and obligations.

I liken this struggle to the concept of object permanence. Object permanence is the understanding that objects continue to exist even when they cannot be observed (seen, heard, touched, smelled or sensed in any way). My challenge with compelling permanence is two-fold: 1) believing the indisputable fact that I am compelling, 2) maintaining that truth even when I'm not getting attention that affirms it. My fear is that if I'm not tending the connection or working every angle to remain available as often as possible, that people in general and Mr. Lucky in particular, will walk away. Summer reminds me that so far with Mr. Lucky, each time there's been any actual or perceived disconnection or distance, he has consistently reconnected with me of his own accord. And she's right. He has. I have no reason to believe he won't again, other than my own fear.

# DEFINE YOUR TERMS

I wish I'd asked Mr. Lucky to clarify whether pressing pause is just for scheduling in-person interactions or whether it means I also won't hear from him via email during this time. Essentially, I wish I'd asked him to define his terms.

He mentioned that he's working to restructure his opportunities for email communication, which leads me to believe that scheduling dates and returning emails are in different categories. It's likely not true that I won't hear from him at all for three weeks.

Lately it takes two or three days to hear back from him, which is an adjustment from the daily volley of emails when we first connected. It took some getting used to (okay, it took some talking me off the proverbial cliff a couple weeks in a row) but now I'm pretty chill about it. I'm headed away for a weekend with my cousins and while it would be nice to hear from him while I'm gone I won't be pining for it. I'll be playing cards and creating memories.

# COUSINS' WEEKEND

Every year as Cousins' Weekend approaches, I dress myself in anxious anticipation – there are snacks to prepare, a countdown until it's time to leave, and a wallet full of dollar bills for the card games. Underneath all that is the longing I was born into, the one dappled into my skin in constellations of freckles. This year, I'll also be dressed in my lucky t-shirt.

All of my siblings will be there – the 8 of us together with most of our first cousins. I'm already sad that three of our brothers are leaving early. I want to hoard them, cling to this togetherness that hasn't even happened yet. Everyone will think my shirt that says *Lucky Me* is about good fortune in the weekend's poker and dice games. Only my sister Tracey knows that it's also about Mr. Lucky.

This weekend is sacred to me – time with my cousins and siblings at one of my favorite places. A place that smells like saltwater and barbecue, that sounds like laughter and the graceful shuffle of cards at the poker table. This is family to me. Hopping from a game of horseshoes on the gravelly beach to dominoes at the kitchen table. The same stories told year after year that knit the blanket of our memories in variegated colors of love and loss, of tragedy and joy.

My own voice is quiet here. I am the baby of my generation, the youngest of twenty cousins. I wrap myself in the vibrant warmth of their stories. I breathe in the sunlight sparkling off the water, listen to the heartbeat of this family, my family. This sweet taste of belonging ought to be enough to distract me from my desire for Mr. Lucky.

*Wed, Jul 31, 2013 at 12:43 PM*
*That's good to hear a pause works for you. It takes some stress off me. Things are all kinds of tense around here. I will need more time before scheduling anything.*

*Hope you're well.*

# EMAIL

Since starting my relationship with Mr. Lucky, I'm extra jumpy whenever my phone makes the droplet sound to alert me that a new email arrived. I checked my phone frequently over the weekend with my cousins. Nothing from him. It's okay, I told myself – I'm having a great time; it's the weekend and he usually writes me during the week from work.

By Tuesday evening I was still edgy every time I heard the water drop sound on my phone, but my emotional experience of this whole thing began to shift. The timing of his needing space is annoying. I'm struggling to believe this has nothing to do with our connection. Yet it really does appear that he's swamped with life and work circumstances, some of which he predicted and communicated to me clearly, and some he didn't see coming.

I want to be compelling enough to him that he couldn't possibly go a few weeks without seeing me. And him needing this break tries to convince me that I am not *enough (*worthy, sexy, interesting, enticing.) Because if I was any of those kinds of enough he would make time to email and see me. And yet, I also know if you don't have it to give, you just don't. I can feel the difference between when he writes from a place of enjoying our banter and when he bangs out a response to quell the pressure of not having responded yet.

I want him to miss me. In my world, missing is a measurement of how much you care about someone. But that's my measurement, not his.

I heard from him today after eight days, the longest span of time with no contact since we met. While the email didn't specifically say he misses me, or offer clear reassurance, it did confirm that he thinks about me. It mostly felt anti-climactic. I was still happy to receive it, but one of my first thoughts was how long it will take to hear back from him when I reply. And that's disheartening. It makes me want to trim my responses to his emails and forgo asking my question. That's not how I prefer to engage with him. I like to be wordy and deliberate and witty instead of drafting austere, curt replies.

It becomes an issue of prioritization. If my primary desire is to write and receive the ideal type of emails, I can choose to focus on that. But if my ultimate goal is sustained, increased contact and deepening connection with him, then I'm better served by responding appropriately to his need for space.

# LONG VIEW

I'm thankful for the relationship I have with my therapist. Gayle and I have worked together off and on for fifteen years. I had no idea when I sought her out that it was even possible to sustain a therapeutic relationship of that longevity. Gratefully, now I know.

Today in therapy I was talking about Mr. Lucky (no big surprise) and how I'm coping with his need for space. I said that mostly I'm doing pretty well with it, but sometimes I get frustrated because I'm generally impatient and I just miss him. Even though most of our connection has been via email, it has been intimate, engaging, and personal. His emails make me laugh, ponder, and look up words I can't define off the top of my head. I feel myself respond on emotional, physical, and intellectual levels and it's alluring.

So here's all of this awesomeness, and yet he needs to pull back. Also present are the clear boundaries that have been drawn around our connection. He has a primary partner and is seeking moderate-commitment connections with other women, which is the category in which I fit. As much as I'm crushed out on him, a long-term primary relationship isn't in the cards for us. Not now, likely not ever. His clarity about that doesn't dilute my reputation for intense attachments in all kinds of relationships, or my desire for him.

Gayle suggested that even though he and I aren't building a primary relationship together, it's still possible that we're crafting a connection with a lifespan of more than a couple months. My struggle to allow for this break might feel different if I approach it from this vantage point. If he and I have the possibility of being intimately connected for a period of many months or even years then what do a few weeks matter? I hadn't allowed myself to imagine long-term potential here because of what I already know is off limits. But what we have together works well. We both enjoy our email exchange. The two dates we've had were sexy and successful. We like each other and are generally compatible. It's inherently possible that this could be a longer-term, casual relationship.

Part of what I'm exploring right now is what sort of relationships I want in my life. My last relationship was technically polyamorous or open, but in practical terms I was monogamous. Right now I'm involved with two men, Mr. Lucky and Matthew, in casual, physical relationships. I don't get as much time with either Mr. Lucky or Matthew as I might like, and neither of them are available for a more serious, romantic partnership. I wouldn't want that with Matthew even if it was possible, but would jump at the chance with Mr. Lucky if it were offered. I'm looking for a primary relationship with a man who is also interested in having other lovers.

If the relationship with Mr. Lucky has the chance to last over time, then Gayle is right: relaxing into this break isn't a big deal. Even if our relationship doesn't endure, my experience of this break will still have been eased by acting as if it will.

# I DON'T WANT TO WAIT

I've sat on the latest email from Mr. Lucky for a couple days now. I don't want to throw it back in his court right away, out of respect for his state of overwhelm. But as I sat down to write him back this evening, I noticed a different thread of reticence in myself. As soon as I craft my response and hit send, I'm waiting for him again. Even if I handle it well and don't freak out about when he'll answer me, I still have to wait. And I just don't want to wait. I can, I will, I have been. But I don't like it.

Sat, Aug 3, 2013 at 1:02 AM
It's good to hear from you.

Relieving some of your stress was part of the plan. I wish there was more I could do to help, aside from supporting your need for space and staying out of the way. I'm sorry to hear about the tension you're experiencing. I trust you'll make it clear when you're able to schedule something.

I'm doing well, thank you. Hope you're hanging in there with all the chaos.

*Fri, Aug 9, 2013 at 10:28 PM*
*i look forward to reconnecting once i get through this crazy
month. next challenge is houseguests (my sister and her
partner) followed possibly by a conference in the UK... then
blessed nothingness.*

*ah, you help, never fear. i have good memories of our
romps, and am definitely growing as a top by reflecting on
them. i sincerely hope you've derived as much value as i
have from this exploration.*

*aye, i will make it clear when i can schedule.*


Mon, Aug 12, 2013 at 12:28 AM
Yes, it will feel good to connect again after the chaos settles.
Blessed nothingness will be such welcome relief for you after all
this.

It feels good to hear that I'm helpful somehow. I wish it could be
more hands on (rather your hands on me, my mouth on you) sort
of help...but there's time for all that when your schedule allows.
My memories of playing together have been useful in this
interim.

I'd really like to hear your reflections on our scenes and how you
are growing as a top. Are you willing to share some of these
thoughts when we see each other? One of my favorite parts of our
email exchange has been talking about the complexities and
psychology of kink. Discussing those ideas in regards to our play
and how it affects each of us (as top and sub, and as individuals)
is exponentially more compelling.

I had an interesting idea for a service-oriented scene the other
day. The top sends his sub a grocery list with instructions to

purchase the groceries before arriving at his house for their scheduled date. The list is mostly food items, with a few suggestive or overtly sexual things mixed in. When she arrives she finds a recipe on the kitchen counter. An apron hangs on a cabinet door with instructions about which pieces of her clothing to remove before donning it. She prepares the meal then serves him dinner and wine, offering herself as a table to eat from if he desires. When he is finished eating, she does all the dishes and tidies the kitchen, refills his wine glass, then settles in front of him to wait for whatever else he has in store for the evening. (This isn't prescriptive, just something I hadn't thought of before in a scene sense. I enjoyed thinking about it.)

# MISSING

Today it's been a month since I last saw Mr. Lucky. In that time I've received four emails from him. I miss him.

I still don't know when I get to see him next. I've been well-behaved and haven't asked. Soon, I hope. He initially said he needed to pause for a few weeks. That was three and a half weeks ago. Yes, I'm counting.

I long for the immediacy of being connected to someone who is truly available. Someone I can text throughout the day or call just to say hi. I want that kind of regular contact with someone I am dating. So far, none of the men I'm involved with are that sort of fit for me. Am I really going to find that by combing dating sites for dates? Is it possible to find a man who wants that with me? I know I'm fun and compelling and attentive and interesting and sexy and compassionate. But when will I find an available, interested, emotionally intelligent man who recognizes that and wants to be attentive to me?

# PERSPECTIVE

Today it occurred to me that Mr. Lucky did in our connection exactly what I didn't choose in my relationship with Clare. He had the foresight to press pause.

In telling the story of that breakup, I often reference how I wish I'd had the awareness to pause when my friend Heather died six months into my relationship with Clare. I was in no place to plan the rest of my life with a new partner as my entire world fell to bits around me.

Mr. Lucky could have walked away, whether he communicated clearly about it or not. He could have attempted to email regularly and set up dates, but not been able to show up in the way we both enjoy and deserve. But he didn't. He took stock of the current situation, anticipated his needs, told me what he could manage, and followed through. A deeper level of acceptance appeared as this sunk in. I still don't like this break. I still want to know when I get to see him again. But this helps me realize that I do feel respected by him and that I do trust his integrity.

Fri, Aug 30, 2013 at 8:21 PM
I'm writing out of turn to share a funny story. On a recent trip to the coast, my best friend's eight-year-old son directed a sandcastle building adventure and handed out jobs to each of us. He asked

me, quite seriously, "Aunt Meg, are you willing to be on your hands and knees?" Summer (the friend I tell everything to) and I busted up laughing; I assured him that yes, I was willing.

I noticed that you took down your dating profile.

I trust you are gracefully navigating the remains of this hectic month. Is there truly an end in sight to all the chaos? I'll admit to feeling a little antsy about scheduling, while still deferring to your authority over it.

# CLARITY OF DESIRE

Over the last week, I've had the chance to talk with many of my closest people about the state of my dating life. Their feedback has been remarkably similar: my current connections aren't working for me.

I definitely want more contact than I'm getting from the men in my life. Even with strong attraction between us and mutual interest in connecting, the limits of time and logistics make it challenging to act on that chemistry. It's been six weeks since I saw Mr. Lucky. Other recent dates have been fun but scheduling is difficult. This begs the question of whether open relationships can give me what I want.

Tonight, I had an inspiring conversation with a friend who described how she specifically sought her latest partner. She clarified what she wanted, including personality, character traits, physical description, and station in life. Now, when she reflects on the man she married and is having a baby with, she realizes he's all of the things she wanted. Maybe I can find what I'm looking for in a similar way. I'd have to become incredibly clear about what I desire in a partner or partners. And then set that intention publicly in as many ways as possible to help make it happen.

I keep being asked whether poly is the right path for me right now. I won't commit to a monogamous relationship because I don't want to lose the chance to play with Mr. Lucky. Friends want to know if that would change if I had a primary partner who met the same needs as my connection with Mr. Lucky. My draw to Mr. Lucky is at least as much about who he is as it is about the type of kink we explore together. Honestly, I think it's slightly more about who he is as an individual than about the play.

My best example of this contrast is Sheldon, my first top. I loved that with Sheldon I got to indulge my curiosity about sex with men as well as BDSM play. But I didn't like him all that much as a person. I didn't crave more time with him or have romantic feelings for him, I just wanted more of the physical release and exploration that he made possible. With Mr. Lucky, I long for more time with him to get to know him and discuss common interests and ideas. Yes, I also want more physical affection and sexual intimacy with him, but that isn't all I want. And I remain clear that I am not likely to get a much of what I am looking for from him, outside of what we've already clearly negotiated.

So even if I found a primary partner who was kinky in similar ways to Mr. Lucky and was also more available, I'd still want to play with Mr. Lucky.

*Wed, Sep 4, 2013 at 7:35 PM*
*hey there! i hope this finds you well. sorry i'm still*
*struggling to find time to write and such.*

*i'll try to organize some thoughts on how this experience is*
*shaping me as a top. maybe i've said this before, but one big*
*benefit has been some concrete self-reflection on what i*
*really enjoy. it's so easy to stop monitoring that and either*
*continue mindlessly in set patterns or miss a chance to*
*explore a new thing... and like any other muscle, kinky*
*creativity needs exercise.*

*another point is becoming more comfortable giving direct*

*orders in scenes. the side benefit to that has been what i consider an improvement in communicating general desires and inclinations (especially to my partner)... i had a lot of training that expressing a preference was essentially rude, when if anything the opposite is true, at least with close friends. i'm talking about things like which flavor of ice cream to buy, you know?*

*your thoughts?*

*ha. good one! aprons are super-hot, too. also he could send her to the hardware store with a list of items that will later be used to restrain/punish/reward her.*

*i've directed a lot of sand castle building workers in my time, usually younger cousins. pretty much the best thing ever. and it was nice of him to ask so politely.*

*yup. kinda a relief to take down my dating profile.*

*i won't be able to schedule until after i return from the UK, which is mid-September. will you remind me of your good days-of-week?*

# THE MYTH OF FINGERPRINTS

Especially after the first time we met, I could feel Mr. Lucky's touch on me throughout the next day. My breath halted as I remembered the smooth command of his hands on my body. With a contented smile on my face, I took a deep breath to savor the memory and incorporate it into my being.

In my fourteen-year marriage I went weeks, months, entire years without sexual contact between us. The reasons for this are complicated. We were physically and sexually aloof. Neither of us actively cultivated that distance, but that was the reality for most of our time together.

Within the last year, my sexual desire has experienced a revival and it's been fun to explore and connect with male lovers. But in the last seven weeks I've had absolutely zero intimate contact with anyone but myself. I'm touch hungry. I crave both the release of sexual play with a partner and the intimacy of cuddling, kissing, caressing that isn't inherently sexual. And I've had none of any of it since the last time I played with Mr. Lucky.

From within this longing for contact my sense memory of lovers' hands on my body falters. The symbolic fingerprints and the response their touch elicits begin to slip away. I want it back. I want more…and soon.

Sat, Sep 7, 2013 at 1:35 AM
Hey! I'm doing well, thanks. I hope you are, too. I'm sorry the time struggle continues.

I'd enjoy casual conversation about what you really enjoy doing and having done. Having this clarity about our real desires feels vital for our own pleasure and that of any partner we play with/date/fuck.

This brings to mind a question: are people you date and people you play with in different, mutually exclusive categories in your world?

I had similar training both in my family of origin and in many of my romantic relationships along the way. Also, in my family, I was steeped in the futility of voicing opinions or exploring individuality at all because of how categorically they were ignored or dismissed.

That is an excellent side benefit and something that I remember you stating that you wanted to improve in your life. Kudos! It sometimes feels, when I refuse to state a preference for where to eat or which movie to watch, that I'm non-consensually bottoming. At the very least, it feels inconsiderate to not be more decisive.

The hardware store idea is great. I like the way you think (but you already know that.)

I can totally picture you directing sand castle construction. It makes me smile.

Thank you, Sir, for confirming about your trip and return date. I appreciate these details.

# APOSTROPHE

I've been participating in Trifecta, a series of weekly writing contests that challenge me to write outside my usual boxes. It's great experience and also connects me to a supportive virtual community of writers. This week's prompt was to write a 33-word apostrophe, which the contest hosts reminded us is where you address an inanimate, absent, or nonexistent thing as if it were here and could understand you. So here's mine, about none other than Mr. Lucky, of course!

You, of the busy schedule and the far-flung business trip...your absence breeds doubt and desire, longing and lassitude. Your words ignite passion. I wait, under pretense of patience, until we meet again.

My favorite comment about it (as a community we read and comment on each other's posts) was *I love the tone of this. I can hear the pout and frustration.* Pout and frustration indeed.

I want to send this to Mr. Lucky. I'll likely wait until it's my turn though.

The best moment of writing this came when the word lassitude popped into my head. I couldn't have defined it in the moment but I knew that was the word to use. I looked it up and found this definition: *a state of physical or mental weariness; lack of energy.* That's one of my most beloved experiences as a writer – when a word descends on me before I can even define it, but I know it belongs.

# INTERNAL ARGUMENT

I'll go ahead and write this now because soon it will be moot.

Tomorrow marks ten weeks since I last saw Mr. Lucky and nine weeks since he asked to pause for a few weeks. It's his turn to write, but I'm antsy. I want to see him again and I fully expect that his next email to me, whenever it arrives, will have details about when we can see each other. Part of me is afraid I'm being a fool, that I need to just walk away to retain my dignity. The voices involved in this internal argument talk over each other all the damn time. It sounds like this:

He doesn't miss you the way you miss him. You're just a plaything he enjoys using on occasion. All your fantasies about dating him are futile, that isn't what he wants or what he is making available to you. Give it up. Either accept what's on the table or move on. Fussing over whether or not to email him out of turn is annoying. You've waited this long, if you truly intend to stick around and take whatever you can get from him, why not wait until he writes you? Yes, he'll enjoy the writing you want to share with him. But it will keep until it's your turn.

So you've been patient. So you've waited three times as long as he said he needed. What do you want? A prize? A sudden shift in what he's offering because you've been a patient, docile creature? Well that isn't likely to happen, now is it?

You calculate when you think you'll hear from him, and each day that goes by without a message makes you feel more foolish. The trouble is, you really don't think he is playing you. You believe him because he hasn't yet broken your trust. So you edit your predictions and play the odds of how long you'll hold out before writing him. You feel a small sense of victory each night as you go to bed that you made it through another day without disturbing the established rhythm of correspondence. And you reassure yourself that you might wake up to find a message from him first thing tomorrow.

If only every single interaction with him didn't draw you in more. Each email feeds your attraction. And spending time in his presence makes you fall that much more for him.

And that's the other fear, that seeing him again will sink you deeper into unrequited attraction. Yes, he respects you and enjoys playing with you. Yes, he likes corresponding. So you're stuck in your same old fear. Do you lay it all out and risk alienating him completely? Do you visibly pout and ask for more from him, knowing the consequence could be he withdraws entirely? Or do you wait, again, still, for him to contact you?

If this is supposed to be the time of blessed nothingness for him— post overseas trip, post partner moving in and then going away for many months, post work firestorm that chewed up his available time for writing—then why hasn't he contacted you yet?

And yes, voice in my head that says repeatedly that he's just not that into me…I hear you. Thanks for your input. I'm going to ignore you from here on out, ok? Nothing personal, I just think you're wrong. He's as into me as he has said he is. If he truly wanted nothing more to do with me, I believe he would clearly state that. It doesn't serve him to keep me dangling here, wanting pieces of him he isn't willing to share. If he was done he would have told me that nine weeks ago. Right?

And really, the one it doesn't serve to be dangling here, wanting pieces of him that he isn't offering, is me. I'm working to reconcile that and figure out what the hell to do about it. So how about a little peace and quiet around here while I do that?!

# RADIO INPUT

I was supposed to have a lunch date but the dude stood me up, again. Last time we were scheduled to have lunch he postponed at the last minute. We texted back and forth a little; I flirted very directly with him and he very clearly did not flirt back with me. When I hadn't heard from him yesterday afternoon, I promised myself that I wouldn't text him to make plans for today. I always initiate contact with him. His replies are quick and engaging, but he never texts first. So I decided to let him reach out about lunch today. And he didn't. I never heard from him. I feel embarrassed for having invested time and energy flirting there. And I feel defeated.

With those feelings fresh within me, mingling noisily with my ongoing Mr. Lucky frustration, I took myself out to lunch – greasy comfort food that's horrible for me but tastes delicious. I turned on the car in time to hear Tom Petty's *The Waiting*. Seriously?! I actually yelled that in the car – seriously universe?! This is what I get? Tom Petty telling me waiting is hard? I told the universe it wasn't funny, except I know it was. Yeah, the waiting is hard. Things with Mr. Lucky would be rosy if there weren't this much waiting. But there is.

I tried to decipher whether this meant I should write Mr. Lucky and ask what gives with his lack of contact, or it means I shouldn't. I think he might appreciate the humor of that moment. And I do think he'll enjoy my apostrophe about him. But if I clearly address my dissatisfaction he might disengage completely, and I don't want that. I also don't particularly want to be in this limbo.

Is there a way to get out of this without input from him? I could decide I'm done. I could decide however long it takes him to re-engage and for us to play again is okay with me. But how do I convince myself of that? I try to create that reality through distraction, by putting myself out there to meet other men. And it isn't working.

After an emotionally raw therapy session with Gayle yesterday, I decided to draft an email to Mr. Lucky. I felt ready to express some of my discontent and inquire about scheduling.


Fri, Sep 27, 2013 at 12:02 AM
I think you'll appreciate this bit of writing I did last week in response to a prompt asking for a 33-word apostrophe…

You, of the busy schedule and the far-flung business trip…your absence breeds doubt and desire, longing and lassitude. Your words ignite passion. I wait, under pretense of patience, until we meet again.

The pretense of my patience is wearing thin. While I appreciate the suspense of waiting for you to command my presence, the reality of ten weeks without seeing you and lack of clarity about when we'll connect again is challenging. Would you please tell me what's happening for you about scheduling?

Hoping you are well and enjoying the blessed nothingness you were anticipating post traveling…


*Sat, Sep 28, 2013 at 7:24 AM*
*i know, i know. i'm sorry to have left you dangling.*

*as numerous unsent drafts testify, i've been struggling to formulate this email. the blessed nothingness of the post-trip period has bred quite a bit of my own lassitude, as well as a striking lack of sexual energy. this state of affairs is compounded by some ill-health and a recent disappointing personal event.*

*i enjoy the play we do but i'm challenged by both my current lack of desire for play and my concerns about the type of connection we are each individually forging. i am wondering if it's wise to continue to play. i do not want to continue to create a situation that leads us further into what i worry are incompatible interests. to wit, i want our connection to be play-only, and i think you are interested in something more holistic.*

*in any case, i should have kept you apprised of this struggle.*

Sat, Sep 28, 2013 at 4:35 PM
Thanks for writing back quickly, I appreciate it.

Thank you for acknowledging that leaving me dangling wasn't the best course of action. With everything going on for you, I now understand the lag time.

I notice myself feeling curiosity, concern, and empathy about each of the things you mentioned. As a friend, and someone who cares about you as a person and is interested in your process, I'd love to hear more.

That we both enjoy the play is indisputable.

I understand that you want our connection to be play-only. Would I want more than that if it was available? (Holistic is apt.)

Undoubtedly. But it isn't. I have no illusion of that, especially after this email from you.

No romance, no dating, no emotional connection beyond that of friendship and what is exchanged during play. What is on the table (which is all that ever was on it) is friendship and scening. That works for me. Truly.

Let's continue to do what we do well together: play as friends. (When you are up for playing again that is.) I honestly don't think it unwise to carry on in this way. The boundaries are clear.

As friends, my ideal hasn't changed since we talked about it post-scene last time. And it's negotiable. I would like to play a game or share a meal with you and talk once a month - not processing our connection, just hanging out, talking about our lives. I'd like to email sometimes to schedule scenes, or share an anecdote, or see how you are, but in a brief, no-pressure way. I'm afraid the email exchange has been a thorn in your side and I don't want that. And I'd like to play one or two times a month, short or long scenes, at your discretion (and your desire).

Also, I am actively seeking a primary partner. Finding one will further ease any extra emotion that is hanging around this connection with you. It won't make you less compelling to me, but I'm capable of channeling that into our play if we get to continue.

Yes, more communication about this struggle would have been helpful. And I get it.

Are you willing to get together for a game and some conversation sometime this week? I would like to see you and talk, please.

# NOT WHAT I WANTED AT ALL, BUT ALSO NOT GIVING UP

What aches in me is how he feeds my words back to me. They must have resonated, spoken to him in all the right ways, for him to repurpose them in his response. That he does this is both beautiful and brutal. This connection through words and our mutual affinity as writers endears him to me in ways I hadn't dared hope for. It makes me wish he was careless with language, that he wasn't accurately attuned. He says he isn't looking to be this emotionally present and yet his writing belies that intention.

Back to waiting, hopefully not for long. I sought some input from Calvin (a therapist friend of mine) and Summer today about my response. And then I just went with it. I wanted my words back in front of him sooner than later, with the hope that we might get to talk within the next week. Re-reading my response, I see that if his meaning of play-only is entirely literal, then he won't be open to my ideas of social connection. I suppose the only way to find out is to wait for his response. At least that's familiar.

*Mon, Sep 30, 2013 at 6:15 PM*
*what a great email! thanks. let me figure out a good day for some games and chat.*

# RELIEF

He wrote back. It was brief and encouraging. And I can breathe again.

The intensity of emotion that shows up for me with Mr. Lucky is not entirely about him. A major part of our connection is about me re-engaging with aspects of myself I've been estranged from for over a decade. I haven't had access to this sort of desire or submission or verbal banter for so long and reconnecting with these parts of myself enlivens me; I feel radiant. Yes, part of it is tied up in how much I enjoy playing with him, but largely it's about feeling alive and present with myself. And this connection with Mr. Lucky also re-ignited my writer self. There's all of this energy, excitement, and engagement with myself that is present in this connection which actually has very little to do with him. I'm eager to explain this all when we get together to talk.

There are a handful of other things I want to communicate to him in person. Most urgent is that if we continue playing together, I need permission to still access the emotional intensity and intimacy that occurs naturally in our scenes. It won't be acceptable for him to shy away from that or shield himself from it, or to expect me to do the same. I need him to not be afraid that any emotionality that comes up during play will spill over outside that context. What we do together in scene is powerful and yes, emotional. I need to be allowed to go all of those places or I don't want to play. And I need him to be willing to experience it in himself as it occurs too. I don't know what emotional impact scening has on him. That will be a good question to explore with him.

I'm relieved at his response. It also seems relief is what he felt after reading my email. I imagine he expected me to be angry or hurt or distraught…all of which I was but I didn't express that to him. I processed the heck out of it elsewhere so as to not visit it on him.

# QUIET ON THE PAGE, NOT IN MY HEAD

Tonight I'm going to Mr. Lucky's house to play a word game and talk. I feel nervous to see him. My friend Calvin keeps teasing me that something more will happen besides a game and chatting, but I need to walk into this situation believing we aren't scening tonight. That isn't an option. I'd really like it to be, considering both times I've seen him in person we've played. (And yes, we've only shared physical space twice.) Just in case, I shaved my legs and chose an outfit that feels sexy and suggestive.

The clarity in my head is loud and I'm nervous about working it all into the conversation tonight. I jotted some notes to bring with me, which feels silly, but I really don't want to forget things. Also, I'm anxious about making small talk. How will I sum up the last eleven weeks of my life without disclosing the turmoil I've been through about him?

# FIRESIDE CHAT

My long day begins when I drop the kiddo off at school slightly late and with her homework for the week incomplete due to a ginormous fuss we had about it yesterday. After three client sessions my noon clients cancel. I take that as an opportunity to get a pedicure. This is an excellent choice for self-care, minus my decision to re-read my entire correspondence with Mr. Lucky while my toes get their workup. My nerves are already frazzled and that doesn't help. My four afternoon client sessions go well, although I'm more distracted than feels right at work. I rush out of the office to get home to my daughter and relieve the new nanny.

Shifting gears from therapist to parent, I navigate the kiddo through bedtime snack, teeth-brushing, pajamas, and a bedtime story. The goal is to get her curly little head on the pillow as close to 7 p.m. as possible. Calvin and his husband agreed to babysit while I go to Mr. Lucky's for the evening. She's almost asleep when the loud squeak of the front door startles her. "Yes," I reassure her, "they're here, now off to sleep." A few minutes later I think she's settled enough to extract myself from the bed but I'm wrong. When I try to sneak out, she whips her head around and demands to know where I'm going. Meekly, I answer, "Nowhere, (yet)." Finally, she falls asleep enough for me to slip out and get dressed for my evening with Mr. Lucky.

Off I go with a dish of apple-pear crisp to share. I'd made it as a thank-you for the boys for watching Frances. It's sweet of them. Especially since Calvin is sick and feels horrible.

When I pull up to Mr. Lucky's house, I see a fire burning in his fireplace. It looks inviting and cozy. I'd had a pep-talk from Summer on the drive over about being my true, authentic self and I take that to heart as I knock at his door. We greet each other with bright smiles, and I hand him the crisp I'd brought. He shakes his head at me, mutters something about me and my gifts. It's true, I don't like to arrive empty-handed. When I ask if I can give him a hug, his affirmative reply is warmly delivered.

He offers me something to drink. We chat about his recent travels, and then we sit on the couch near the fire and talk. And talk. And talk. It takes us both a bit to warm up socially, although I'm way less fidgety than I feared. It feels natural to be in his presence. The conversation is lively and engaging, reciprocal and full of curiosity. Without consulting my notes, I casually work my way through everything I need to say.

After a bit, we switch gears to start a game. The game is fun – lots of talking, both casual and more intense, over the board. We share anecdotes about our lives, our families, the one friend we have in common. We discover a shared love of card games and I ask whether he plays dominoes.

"You seemed relieved at my email," I venture.

"Yeah, I forced myself to read what you wrote and was incredibly relieved. I told myself, *Right, Meg understands. I can just be honest with her.*"

I smile in response. He gives what I suspect is his usual line about getting all the good letters. I tease him about just being gracious, which he jokes is easy to do when you're winning. At some point his cat comes into the room and joins us at the table. They share a sweet nose-to-nose moment that very nearly melts my heart, and I say so. He laughs.

There's a moment of embarrassment about my inability to count on the fly. I try to add up points for a word I play and I get it all wrong.

I hold on to myself though, without spiraling into shame about this shortcoming. "Numbers trip me up like that sometimes. I'm great with words, but counting aloud is often my downfall," I explain.

He's friendly about it and doesn't dismiss me. "Why do you think that's true for you?" he asks.

"Mostly, I'm trying to move too fast. If I slow down I can usually do it." I feel like I'm under a microscope the rest of the game each time I add my points. When I mess it up again he's gentle and encouraging. It feels sweet.

After the game, which he wins, of course, we settle back on the couch for more talking. "So what exactly is so challenging for you about the emails I send?" I ask.

"Your desire to know so much about me feels almost as like an attempt to subsume me." It's such a vivid description of how the excess intensity affects him. I completely understand how it could impact him that way and am so grateful for him saying it. "It's rare for me to talk at both this length and this depth, with someone that isn't my partner." I smile at that. "It feels good to talk with you. I enjoy this. It just also feels foreign."

Earlier in the evening we talked about hobbies and I admitted that I often struggle to answer questions about my interests. "Really I think what we're doing right now is my hobby. Being together, talking, laughing, sharing stories."

He laughed and said, "I get the feeling you could leave from an evening like this and go off into the night to have another long conversation with someone else."

"Yes!" I confirmed. "In fact, if my friend Calvin who is watching my daughter wasn't sick and asleep on my couch, I likely would go home and talk with him for an hour about how tonight went."

"And he would want to know?!?" Mr. Lucky is astounded.

"Yeah, but he's a therapist too," I explain.

This kind of intimacy is the norm with my friends. I tell him how me and Summer, after 27 years of knowing each other, still mostly just sit and talk when given the chance. This seems to solidify the point for him. It doesn't mean he can relate, but at least he understands.

"I assume anyone who wants to know this much about me must be falling in love with me," he says.

We talk about the specifics of how and when we'll spend time together in the future. I ask if the ideas I laid out in my email were acceptable to him. "I think so," he says. "That periodicity feels right to me." I love that he drops words like that in our conversations. Thankfully, he didn't also play it during our word game. We make a date to scene in two weeks – a brief lunch hour rendezvous. He muses, "I appreciate the depravity of coming home at lunch during my work day to play with you and then return to work." I undoubtedly like it too.

As we consult our calendars to make plans, he says something about how this gives us a chance to touch our phones. "Well, we aren't touching each other," I note. "We might as well have our hands on something." I tell him Calvin didn't believe that we were only going to talk and play a game, but that I'd been clear that I had to enter this situation believing nothing else was going to happen.

Mr. Lucky agrees. "Although it's tempting, because after all we're both already here and we both enjoy it." I like that he's tempted. Earlier in the evening over the board game, I asked whether we would get to scene again. "Yes," he answered. "Nothing wrong with the play at all. No one is saying that!" That's my favorite thing he said all night.

It feels good to have cleared the air by talking freely and openly. I struggle to keep from laughing when he says that as much as he's enjoyed our conversation, he's afraid his throat might actually be a little sore from all the talking.

Just after midnight, I force myself to leave. I don't want Calvin and Adam stranded at my house forever. We share another warm hug on my way out that definitely conveys sexual energy. He asks if he can keep the crisp that was leftover, but wants to give me back the container. "It's okay," I say, "I'll be back."

"Oh right! Well isn't that handy?!"
Yes, indeed it is.


Sat, Oct 5, 2013 at 9:12 PM
This email contains absolutely zero subsuming, guaranteed.

Thanks for a really fun night last night. The fire, the talking, the game, all of it was lovely.

Thank you for pushing yourself to read my email response, make plans to see me, and talk as openly, honestly, and as much as you did.

I appreciate the effort and enjoyed your company. All in all, a fantastic way to spend an evening with a friend.

Maybe dominoes next time? (Sometime when we hang out without scening again, suggested with no urgency about planning or scheduling, at all. None.)

# WHY ISN'T THE CONFIDENT VOICE MY LOUDEST?

I almost always feel like too much, except when I'm afraid I'm not enough. Today Calvin reflected that almost any action I take immediately starts an internal conversation about how it will be interpreted. Am I too much or not enough? Did I do something wrong or displease the other person? "I know!" I replied. Why isn't the confident voice my loudest? Why don't I hear a voice that says, *You did great! That was a really good move, you did it right, you were as funny and engaging and attuned and interesting and compelling as you intended and the other person is delighted by you.*

The last email I sent Mr. Lucky is a good example. I wanted to send a brief friendly thank you for the evening together. It needed to be clear that I wasn't seeking anything from him. My email met all of my goals. And yet I've felt anxious since sending it. What if he's upset that I said I was going to back off from email, and yet wrote him the very next day?

I want to act from a place of confidence and to reassure myself when these doubts creep in. I long for the presence of mind and strength of heart to trust that I've represented myself well. I crave certainty of where things stand with the other person. With Mr. Lucky things were left on pretty damn good ground. We both enjoyed the evening, and we scheduled a date to scene. We shared a warm, intense embrace as I was leaving and parted on friendly terms. What the hell am I worried about?

*Thu, Oct 10, 2013 at 5:44 PM*
*i appreciate the lack of subsuming!*

*dominoes sounds like a plan at some point.*

# INTEGRAL

I just read this essay and this paragraph felt like it was written from my own marrow:

> "You won't find integral as a synonym for beautiful in any thesaurus. In my vocabulary, they share meaning. Integral means both whole and essential to the whole. If you are integral, you are complete, and the world would not be complete without you. What I have learned over years of reflection is that when I long to be beautiful, I long to be integral." – Kim Kankiewicz, *Eye of the Beholder*

It used to just be darlin'. Nearly every time we greeted each other, in person, by phone, or in writing, that was how Summer and I referred to each other. Somehow over the last year or more, darlin' has shifted and expanded into a list which includes the words beautiful and gorgeous, along with usual terms of endearment like sweetheart. Until reading those words linking integral and beautiful, it never made sense why these greetings felt both resonant and discordant. The dissonance comes from what has always felt true: when she calls me gorgeous, she isn't referring to my physicality as such, in the way of conventional beauty standards. What she means is the stunning quality of who I am as a person, and as one of her people. She is calling out to the me who is essential in her life. Our being integral to one another is undeniable.

As I wrestle with the idea of being or wanting too much, I'm soothed by this concept of longing to be integral. In my recent dating adventures, I've had moments of feeling beautiful, sexy, and desirable. But I have never felt integral. With each of these men I have been expendable. Even if we like each other or the sex is good or we share similar interests, no one has expressed that he finds me necessary or essential in his life.

# I ACTUALLY DON'T UNDERSTAND

There's something about moderation that I just don't understand. I'm not wired for it. One reason I don't drink alcohol is because I drink too much of whatever is in my glass, so if the beverage was alcoholic and I liked the taste of it (I mostly don't, which is the other reason I don't imbibe) I would drink it to excess. Technically that's theoretical, but I take it as fact.

Mr. Lucky and I enjoy time together as friends. And we like scening together. So why wouldn't we want to see each other more often?

Searching for something I wrote to Mr. Lucky on a dating site, I noticed he started up his profile again. *Holy mixed reactions, Batman!* Partly I'm relieved; things must be improving for him to connect with new people. But I also feel kicked in the gut. He's looking for other partners but doesn't want more connection with me?! So again, why moderation? I'm not saying let's hang out every day, but why not connect more if we like what's here?

This is an ongoing, multi-person issue for me. I want more connection than people seek from me. It's been a long time since I have been the sought after one. It would have been easy to say it has never happened, but that isn't true. It's just rare and fleeting.

It comes down to this: I just don't get tired of people I like. Friends, romantic interests, family members…if I enjoy your company or some shared activity with you, chances are good that I want to do more of that with you or do it with you more often.

# LUNCH HOUR – SCENE NUMBER THREE
### October 16, 2013

*Wednesday you'll arrive at my house at 12:30pm.*

*You'll enter the house, close all the blinds in that front room, and lock the door.*

*You'll strip to your skirt and your socks (so wear a skirt and your longest socks and don't bother with underwear). Nothing else.*

*You'll collar yourself, then kneel in front of the couch and rest your head on the seat. Put your hands behind your back and relax. Wait for my arrival. Relax.*

*When I enter the room, acknowledge my presence by hiking up your skirt to expose your cunt and ass.*

*I will tell you when to perform your ritual of submission and instruct you from there.*

I walk up the driveway to let myself into the house at precisely 12:30 p.m. and set to work on the blinds. One of them outsmarts me with thick wooden slats that won't cooperate. It seems simple enough, but I can't get it to close no matter what I try. Panic roosts in my chest. I walk away from the troublesome window to close the remaining blinds and lock the door. I try one more time. When I pull the cord to lower it the shade rises instead. *Fuck! Now what?*

My only option is to text him. He hates text messages, but I don't know what else to do. *Sir, I can't close one of the blinds. Help!* His response doesn't come quickly enough, so I abandon the task and follow the rest of his commands.

Putting on my own collar offends my devotion to submission. A collar should only be placed and removed by a Top. But my role is to obey him without question. His collar for me is made of smooth leather in two colors with one silver ring attached in the center. My fingers tremble as I slide one end through the silver buckle to fasten it in place. Nervous. Excited. Hungry for his touch.

Kneeling in my short black skirt and charcoal grey knee socks, my head rests on the light green upholstered couch cushion. My hands are clasped at my back. I am not relaxed; my every nerve anticipates his key in the lock.

He arrives home (after a few minutes that feel like an hour), unlocks the door, and enters the room. Wordlessly I raise my skirt as instructed. "What a lovely sight," he remarks. I grin into the couch, more at the sound of his voice than the compliment. He walks directly to the blind I wasn't able to close; it obeys his touch the first time, just as I will.

At his command I face him. He's wearing a light blue button-down shirt with a striped tie, paired with his signature Lucky Brand jeans. He watches me flush with desire as I adjust to his presence. "You may begin the ritual now."

We lock eyes as I recite, "While I am here, I am yours to use in any way you choose, Sir." My submission is punctuated by a kiss to his foot.

"Continue kissing my feet." As I resume the task I reach back to lift my skirt again. "Now you're improvising. No one told you to do that…" His reprimand sizzles through my body. I quickly smooth my skirt back down.

"That's so slutty," he says, clearly enjoying my tongue on his toes. "And you do it with such enthusiasm!"

He nudges me forward onto my hands and knees to examine my half-naked body. His hand traverses my back possessively, navigating the delicious curve of my ass before sliding two fingers inside me. I respond with a sharp intake of breath followed by silence. He grabs a fistful of my hair, pulls it firmly towards him.

"You're holding your breath. Why?"

When my answer isn't immediate, he abruptly removes his fingers from within me. I exhale in a whimper, desperate about this sudden vacancy.

"I wasn't sure if relishing your inspection was permitted, so I chose not to broadcast my pleasure, Sir."

He releases my hair and orders me back up on my knees. "Your abundant wetness gives you away, slut."

I blush. "Yes, Sir,"

"Who owns your arousal?" he snaps.

"You, Sir. My body, my desire, and my arousal all belong to you, Sir."

With his hand under my chin he tilts my face up until my green eyes meet his stern gaze. "That was a good, comprehensive answer. Pay attention. I'll only say this once: you are not allowed to disguise any aspect of your arousal in my presence. Is that clear?"

His words reverberate through my chest, pulsing in my cunt. The uninhibited moan they elicit is likely sufficient in response, but I manage to also stammer, "Yes, Sir. Perfectly clear."

He continues to explore my body while interrogating me. "When was the last time you were fucked?" He pinches my nipples until I wince, then releases them.

"Since the last time I was with you, Sir. So about twelve weeks."

He walks behind me and shoves me forward onto all fours again. "And the last time you sucked cock?"

"About three weeks ago, Sir."

"How'd you do?" This question renders me momentarily speechless. I'm relieved he can't see me blush.

Eventually I answer, "I did OK, Sir. He seemed to enjoy it." His laughter flusters me.

"I'd rather have been sucking your cock, though, Sir." Talking out of turn might get me in trouble but I can't seem to stop myself.

"That's nice of you to say," he responds.

*Whew! Not in trouble for the moment.* "I'm not saying it to be nice, Sir. I'm saying it because it's true." *Why am I still talking?*

"Why would you rather suck my cock?"

"You're more attractive, Sir and I like you better."

He doesn't respond to this flirtatious adoration. "I'm going to the kitchen to make my lunch. You will stay here and cut this apple into bite sized pieces." He gestures toward a cutting board, apple, and paring knife on a low table nearby. I crawl over to begin my work as he leaves the room.

He returns about five minutes later carrying a glass of water and a plate of hot food. There's a rolled-up magazine tucked under his left arm. I'm not sure whether the magazine is to read or for hitting me. Perhaps both. Sir sits down on the couch. "Come here, slut. You'll be my table."

I position myself on hands and knees in front of him. He sets the plate on my naked back and balances the glass of water beside it. My body registers the contrasting temperatures. Warm plate. Cold water glass. The magazine rests by my shoulders. I smell garlic and butter. "What's for lunch?" I ask.

"Aren't you forgetting something?"

"Oh, right. What's for lunch, *Sir*?" I try again, slow to remember his honorific.

"Pierogi," he answers. "They're like potato dumplings. Simple and delicious." I smile to myself. Pierogi are one of my favorite foods. I add this to the exhaustive mental list I maintain of things we have in common.

He reaches for the magazine, unrolls it, and makes a show of rustling the pages while he eats. I wait, hungry for him. I try to hold still but I'm restless. I want serving him this way to satisfy me but I'm anxious for what else he has planned.

When he's done eating, he moves the plate and glass from my back. "If you need to use the bathroom, now's your chance," he offers.

"Yes, thank you." When I look at him, he appears to be waiting for something. "Sir. Thank you, Sir." He doesn't need to chastise me, I'm embarrassed enough that I keep forgetting.

When I return, he's on the couch with a coil of red rope beside him. "Kneel here so I can tie this harness on you." I drop to my knees facing him. He threads the rope under my breasts and behind my back, making a figure eight pattern that functions as a harness. He's struggling with the rope and he's frazzled but doesn't want me to notice.

"I've never seen you in your work clothes before. You look good, Sir."

"I look okay," he answers, distracted.

"Oh, and modest I see?!"

"One has to be modest when they are failing at this kind of rope task."

This moment challenges me to stay in my role as his submissive, and not shift into my role as therapist. I feel his disappointment and want to reassure him. But he's not interested in my empathy. He just wants to finish this tie and continue the scene.

He gives up, tosses the rope aside. "Stand up. Go to the shelf at the end of the hallway and retrieve the stack of bills. Bring it here, along with the stamps beside it." I do as I'm told and return to my knees before him.

His pants are pulled down and his cock is directly in my line of sight. I maintain my composure as desire courses through me. "You'll worship my cock while I pay these bills, slut. If I have to pay bills, I might as well get a blow job while I do it."

I'm incredulous. *He teaches computer science, an ultimate geek. Why does he pay bills on paper? But if it means I get to suck his cock, I'm not complaining.*

I dive into the blow job, trying to remember his previous instructions. It's been months since I served him this way. I'm out of practice. He writes checks for his utility bills, only engaging with me to direct my movement. "I expect you to take more than that. Stay there."

I'm getting tired but he shows no sign of climax. He sets the bills aside, pulls me off his cock by my hair. "Turn around, slut." When I do, he pushes me onto my belly and shoves his fingers inside me. "Is this what you want, bitch? Have you been thinking about this since I sent you those instructions?"

"Yes, Sir. I want you to fuck me."

"What about the instructions I sent captured your attention?"

"Being told what to wear and what not to wear. Collaring myself. Waiting for your arrival."

"What did you think about collaring yourself?"

"I was conflicted," I admit. "But it's what you wanted, so I did it."

He pulls his fingers out of my cunt. "Turn around and open your mouth."

I face him and he slides both slippery fingers into my mouth. I wait, mouth open, for further instructions. With his other hand, he grabs the ring at the front of my collar. "You're damn right it's what I wanted."

My insides clench where his fingers just were. I moan at his words. "Suck these fingers clean, slut." I transfer all my desire for him fucking me into this task of cleaning my juices off him. When he's satisfied, he orders me to lay down on my back. He kneels over me, dangling his hard cock near my mouth. I shift toward it without waiting for permission. He slaps my face, hard. This doesn't deter me.

"Such a greedy slut today," he teases. He lowers himself above me so his cock slides into my mouth. The position is awkward, and I can't take him very deep. He seems frustrated which makes me anxious. I just want to please him. And I want him to cum. He changes position several times before sitting back on the couch with me on my knees before him.

I can tell he's close to climax. His approach is silent, but I feel his body tense. He lets me catch my breath, asks, "where do you want my cum?"

"Anywhere you want to give it to me," I defer. But he pushes.

"Beg me for my cum, slut. Tell me where you want it."

"Please, Sir, I want your cum in my mouth. I want to taste you. Please Sir." My begging is uninspired but it works. With one final long pull on his cock he releases into orgasm. I try not to gulp down the cum as I gasp for breath. I'm relieved when he grants me permission to swallow.

I rest my head on his thigh and he runs his hand through my hair. He finally seems relaxed. We linger not nearly long enough; he's got to get back to work. "Is it time to take this off now, Sir?" I ask, referencing the collar still clasped around my neck.

"Oh yeah, let me do that." He unbuckles the collar to officially end the scene. We debrief a bit as we each put clothes back on. He bemoans the rope mishap and won't accept my assurance that it wasn't a total loss. We joke about my forgetting to address him as Sir. More than once he mentions the next time we'll play, and every time he does my insides rearrange themselves. *We get to play again!* He hugs me goodbye before we walk out the door and I watch him walk down the block with a satisfied smile.


Thu, Oct 17, 2013 at 8:03 AM
Good morning, Mr. Lucky. I hope you enjoyed the rest of your day yesterday.

I don't know about you, but I found it challenging to focus at work after our scene.

I need some feedback about yesterday. Could you make time to have a brief conversation or written exchange about it in the next day or two? I'm not freaking out, but I have some concern about my performance. If we'd had more time yesterday to debrief, it likely would have come up then. But our time flew by and there was work to return to. If you're willing, please let me know how you prefer to interact about it. Thanks!

*Thu, Oct 17, 2013 at 4:32 PM*
*sure thing. i've been doing some processing as well. let's exchange thoughts over email and see how that goes. you first!*

Thu, Oct 17, 2013 at 10:23 PM
Thanks again for being willing to engage more about our scene. I'll attempt to be brief.

First and foremost I had a great time; it felt incredible to submit to you again. I respect and appreciate the planning you put into these scenes. I hope you're getting a good return on that investment from our play. (That sounds more cold and clinical than I mean.)

Driving across town in a skirt with no panties, at your instruction, felt so sexy. I might have been wet before arriving at your place just from this.

My primary concern about yesterday centers around sucking your cock. My fear is that I failed; that my performance of that quintessentially submissive act was dismal and disappointing to you on many levels. We both know I have all the eagerness in the world for this task (which you appear to find amusing and I hope is also hot for you). I know that my desire to suck your cock in the way you expect it makes me nervous and that gets in the way of me doing it right.

Part of this is my lack of experience, and the absence of clear direction from previous tops. I want to be able to take your cock in exactly the way you give it to me, for as long as you want to fuck my mouth, without gagging or choking, without struggling (recognizing that watching me struggle, choke, or gag might be part of your desire). I want to be able to hold your cum as long as you expect me to before swallowing, and to not spill any of it. And I failed at those parts too. I swallowed too soon, not out of disrespect or insubordination, but from reflex. I disappointed you (I fear) and in doing so disappointed myself. I expected to be slapped in the face for that failure, and I imagine if you hadn't been so crunched for time, you might have - just like you would have made an issue about my being late saying Sir when addressing you.

The smart-ass, impertinent sub in me wants to add that if I hadn't had to wait so damn long in between scenes with you, we'd have gotten further on my cock-sucking training regimen by now.

Your question of how I did sucking that other guy's cock was a well-played Dom question that I didn't expect.

Any timely feedback you're willing to give about your experience of yesterday's blowjob will be very useful. I can handle (and desire) blunt, honest feedback.

Previously, this perceived failure would have made me wonder whether we'd play again. I'm not feeling that fear this time. There was enough mention of next time, and things we want to try together in the future that I feel mostly at ease about the idea that we will play again. (It's going to suck if I'm wrong about that.)

I'm curious about your experience of this shorter scene (and anything else you're willing to share about our scene or the processing you've done since). I really liked you arriving to find me waiting for you as instructed (and your comment about it being a nice sight to come back to did wonders to soothe my nerves.) I wished we'd had more time, but also appreciated the extra intensity of the time limit. Watching you stroll down the block to work after we played was pretty damn awesome.

# VOICE

Today my impatience about receiving a response back from Mr. Lucky almost swallowed me whole. I was irritable, jumpy, anxious. I decided to take matters into my own words and write myself a reply in my perception of his voice. My intention wasn't to necessarily write the response I wanted from him but some approximation of what I expected he'd write. I think it ended up as a mix of the two. It calmed me down enough to go on with my day. The voice I ascribed to him was rough and mean. I think that's my fear talking.

Meg-
That wasn't brief. <joking>.

So you're afraid that you suck at sucking my cock. You didn't fail. You sucked me off and swallowed my cum. Really how bad could it have been?

There is still learning to be done in order to perform this task to the standard I demand of you. I, too, am invested in you becoming proficient at this in service to me – if I have to pay bills, I want you worshiping my cock while I do. Your performance is not something that will disqualify you from serving me again in the future. Your submissive desire to perfect sucking my cock is hot to me. Your nervousness not so much. And I concede the point to your smart-ass comment...yes, playing regularly, without a three-month break, would facilitate this learning. Also, having more time in a scene would help.

Many aspects of our play this week worked for me. Some did not.

-Your perception of Mr. Lucky

*Fri, Oct 18, 2013 at 9:22 PM*
*wow, you can really turn out some prose!*

*eh, it's a clinical topic. thus far the ROI has been acceptable.*

*a skirt with no panties is a classic. i'm glad it worked for you.*

*well, that kind of desire to please me is really all one can ask. and i have not felt much insubordination from you at any time. but i do expect you to improve your technique. more below.*

*(by the way, you used one of my negative trigger words: dismal. i hate that one! please don't use it about yourself.)*

*i agree that question about you sucking the other guy's cock was a good moment. it brings up a point that relates to all the above, which is that i was only barely satisfied with my topping. the combination of time pressure and my recent struggle to connect with my sexual energy was a tough row to hoe. in the end i was unhappy because i played the scene wrong. i should've followed a more relaxed and sensual vibe, rather than semi-stern taskmaster or whatever i aimed for and missed. the vibe would've been good and i think i'd have found more creativity. and the rope debacle bothered me more than i could at first admit. i couldn't shake the feeling of wasting your time, which is not very dom for one thing, and made me tense for another...*

*cock sucking review: you need to chill out and not try to go 100% all the time. you need a lot of your muscles, from your lips and tongue to your jaws and neck, to be more relaxed. your tongue in particular is good, but you only use it one way. it should sometimes be soft and used for auditory effect, and then other times firm and used for friction. in general you should allow more saliva to build up for a pleasing slurping sound. most certainly you need to figure out how to ensure that your teeth don't touch my cock, or at least only rarely and lightly. in the more advanced class, you need to work on taking depth, and on being comfortable gagging and choking. your neck should be flexible and loose enough that i can position and move your head as i wish, without using force.*

*on my part, i generally would have guided you much more slowly and informatively, although i did want to test you by going directly to a more intense style. i didn't do it how i wanted and i partially blame my poor time management.*

*also, my struggle to achieve a topping energy limited my disciplinary effectiveness. that will be resolved in the future.*

*got to run!*

Sat, Oct 19, 2013 at 12:52 AM
Thank you for responding so quickly. I appreciate you making time to write back today. Your reflections are so helpful.

Yeah, I'm a wordy whore. Perhaps I need a word count max instead of a one question per email limit (which in this exchange I am not heeding, because we're debriefing the scene). Word count requirements seem to work well in my writing for craft.

Acceptable...hmm, not a glowing assessment.

Knowing you don't like to punish, I haven't pushed back. I like the idea of challenging the authority of my top, but I am generally a well-behaved slut.

Yes, Sir. I want to improve my technique too, for both our sakes.

Technically I used dismal to describe my performance, not myself. And...noted. I won't use it.

Damn, I'm sorry to hear our scene was a challenge for you. Within this struggle, what have you found that reliably connects you with your sexual energy?

That relaxed and sensual vibe sounds delightful, given how long it had been since we'd played, it seems that could have felt like getting reacquainted. Can we please scene sometime with this vibe?

The sense that you're wasting my time sounds awful. It resembles how I felt when sucking your cock. Thank you for admitting that the rope thing bothered you. I figured it did, but didn't push it in the moment because I didn't want to overstep. I hear that you felt unhappy and tense about how you played the scene and I can really imagine how disappointing that would be.

I didn't, for a second, feel like my time was wasted. When I submit to you I am exactly where I want to be...vibrantly at home in my body, feeling sexy and desired, in the presence of a strikingly handsome, sexy, wickedly smart, attuned, engaging, compelling, creative, dominant man who is paying me attention, desiring and commanding me. Nothing about that experience feels like a time waste at all, regardless of whether the rope bondage (or whatever else you have planned) works out.

I am so grateful for this review, Sir, you have no idea. Seriously useful. Aside from more live practice on you, what demands or requests do you have for how I figure this out? Homework assignments welcome. Even though we clearly aren't in a 24/7 dynamic, this is something I will be working on to better serve you. I just will. I have a dildo I practice on at home. Your direction is respectfully requested.

I didn't know it would be good to make slurping noises or that there should be an auditory effect while sucking your cock. I tend toward hyper-self-consciousness about sounds during sex, because I get loud and unless I know for sure that my partner gets off on it, I feel embarrassed. You always seem amused when your touch elicits noises of pleasure from me. Am I reading that correctly? Do you enjoy that I'm noisy?

One suggestion for when we play during your work day again - could it be part of my instructions to pick up lunch for you on the way to your house, or to arrive early enough to prepare food for you?

When can we see each other again - to scene or play dominoes? I know we often look at least a week or two out to find a time that fits in both of our schedules. Did this first experience turn you off from lunch time scenes?

I apologize for the length of this email. I actually do try to be brief, and I do edit and leave stuff out. I am not attempting to start an intense, ongoing exchange the likes of which we had previously. Thank you again for respecting my need for feedback and for your responsiveness even when things are busy for you. I feel less urgency than before, so waiting a little bit works for me in response to this email.

(p.s. - I was going to send this attachment in a separate email tomorrow but since it is 2 a.m. it's already your birthday, so there you go. Hope the day is great.)

# TIRED OF MYSELF

I am about to put myself to bed, hoping I wake up in a better mood tomorrow. Today I mostly felt tired of myself. I was cranky and irritable and snapped at my daughter all afternoon. I told Summer it might be PMS, which is weird because my cycles are so irregular. She replied, "Right, and you've already bled this year..." She's funny; talking to her always makes me feel better.

I'm annoyed at all the fuss I make about Mr. Lucky. Calvin calls him 'the dude', and it helps me remember that he is just a dude who is my friend. At lunch with one of my brothers today I caught myself referring to Mr. Lucky as the guy I'm seeing. I need to stop that. He isn't a guy I am seeing, unless I'm talking about him as a play partner. Then I can use accurate language to describe our connection. Otherwise, he's my friend.

I adore the play that we do; I appreciate what I'm learning about myself through this process. I think he's pretty awesome. And I'm sort of tired of being so wrapped up in it. Partly, this stems from knowing that if I chose to walk away from this connection, I would likely be devastated. But he wouldn't. He's not as involved in this dynamic as I am. He might miss me a little bit, but he wouldn't pine for me or be distraught.

# TAKE THIS MEANNESS OUT OF ME

It's difficult to escape this mean voice inside my head. I noticed it first when I wrote that response to myself as if it was from Mr. Lucky. It won't leave me alone.

I've thought about writing another pretend response like that, to the last email I sent him. But I just hear the mean voice saying things like, "You're exhausting. You want to process everything to death."

I'm working on Mr. Lucky just being a friend I play with sometimes instead of someone I'm eternally obsessing over. I feel ready for that shift, but it hasn't ground itself into gear yet. Waiting for that makes me grumpy as hell.

I'm also just ready for a boyfriend. I am ready to meet someone who wants to spend time with me and is available to do that. This lonely longing for connection is exhausting. Folks keep encouraging me that it will happen. I really want to believe them.

Earlier today I saw a post on Facebook about whether our presence in other people's lives is a gift or a burden. When I told Summer about it, she asked whether I believe that any offering of myself is a gift, not a burden. I said yes, in regards to her but not globally in my life. Like with Mr. Lucky (our ever-present example)…unless I'm stepped quite far back from the situation, I don't think my presence in his life is a gift. I'm inclined to say I am a burden. And yet I know, logically, that he would stop interacting with me if that were the case.

# WHILE I AM WAITING

It's interesting to be once again waiting to hear back from Mr. Lucky, while also trying to chill the fuck out about our connection. Although a tiny bit of me wants to run the same fear narratives I usually do, mostly I'm doing okay. I'm curious whether he's willing to continue this dialogue in a meaningful way. But I don't really think I've said too much, or that I'm asking for anything that would cause him to end the connection. If he feels like I'm out of bounds, he can tell me that. But that doesn't mean that my actions were inappropriate.

I told him I was not feeling urgent and could wait a bit for his response. Of course I'll wait for his reply as long as it takes him to send one. I did ask when we can see each other again. He'll write back when he does and it will likely all be fine. At some point it really will happen that my inbox will show a new email from him. I will thrill about it and read it many times over and life will move on.

It's important to remember that just because I haven't received an email from him yet doesn't mean he isn't working on it. He seems to chip away at his replies piece meal over many days before sending them. I might not see him as soon as I want, but I imagine that we will scene again. Our debrief feels like two people working out what happened in the context of how to do it differently in the future. No one even hinted at the idea that there won't be a next time.

Maybe he would commit to a contract of sorts—agree to play three more times and then re-evaluate—so I don't walk away from every scene worried that it's the last. It helps to know when I leave his house when I'll see him again. Even if it's weeks away, knowing I'm in his calendar is reassuring.

And I really need to step up my efforts to find a primary partner.

*Thu, Oct 24, 2013 at 11:13 PM*
*i'm on a laconic kick. but feel free to write as much as you like. i wasn't curtailing.*

*yeah, for now i think near-absolute and prompt obedience should be our game.*

*technical point noted and my objection to the word dismal is withdrawn. but that's how trigger words are, they unbalance the judgment center. i hate the hopelessness of that word.*

*might could, as they say. i have thoughts about scening with that energy.*

*i appreciate hearing that you didn't feel your time was wasted.*

*oh certainly. aural reactions are pleasant and important. got to use as many senses as possible!*

*i'm not comfortable with your bringing me food. it crosses a boundary for me – mixing play with essential life functions or such.*

*nope - i don't often get discouraged. it actually made me eager to try another lunchtime scene for contrast. there's certainly stuff to be learned. how about midday 10/30?*

*thanks for the attachment, no pun intended.*

Fri, Oct 25, 2013 at 11:27 AM
Good to know. I don't want to impose on your time or attention with too many words.

Yes, Sir. Prompt obedience, as you wish.

I like that you objected and your descriptions of why you did so. I refute your withdrawal. The objection stands.

My they don't say *might could*. They might start now.

I will respect and defer to your boundary about food, but I don't see it the same way. It feels service-oriented to me, and friendly. But it isn't my call.

I will anticipate instructions from you early next week.

# SWIMMING

On a walk with Calvin today I mentioned that I heard from Mr. Lucky and that we get to play again next week. I tried out my downshifting theory on him; he was skeptical. He could see that I want to believe Mr. Lucky is just my friend and a dude I play with sometimes. But he didn't buy that I've achieved this state.

Calvin offered a different metaphor. He suggested that my current mode is like being in the water up to my neck but claiming that I'm not totally wet. *See?! My head is dry. The inside of me is still dry!* I couldn't argue with him. What I want is to interact with Mr. Lucky as an experience of jumping in the water full force. I need to let myself feel it completely. But then I have to get out of the water, dry off, and go do something else just as fully. Otherwise I linger in the water and end up soggy with pruney fingers. I want to submerge myself in the connection with him in discrete encounters, not languish there in an exhausting cycle of experience - analysis – writing – dialogue – disconnection – hopelessness – reconnection…

*Tue, Oct 29, 2013 at 11:32 PM*
*Last-minute instructions*
*Arrive at 1pm, having eaten.*

Wear jeans or something similar. There's no need for underwear. Wear your lowest-cut shirt. Ideally your tits should be practically falling out of it, but do your best. A jacket over top of this is a good idea.

Come to the front door and knock. I'll be there already.

We'll have a brief hello and I'll tell you when to begin the ritual.

# SECOND LUNCH — SCENE NUMBER FOUR
## October 30, 2013

*When you ordered me to write about this scene, I don't think you gave specific directions about what sort of writing you expect: polished, erotic, feedback, stream-of-consciousness reflections. If you were explicit, I didn't catch it. You just said to write about my experience. This became a mix of all of the above. I hope it suffices.*

I arrive ready to play so our brief greeting seems like an interruption somehow. I'm relieved he's already closed the blinds; I didn't want him to watch me fumble with them.

Before reciting my ritual opening, I notice him staring at my tits. Is *this low-cut enough? Do my tits spill over the way he wants?* Our eyes meet as I recite my vow of submission, "While I am here, I am yours to use in any way you choose, Sir." I break our eye contact to lean over, kiss his foot and wait for further instructions.

The ritual continues to ground me in our dynamic and drop me quickly into sub space.

"Lay on the couch here, with your head in my lap," he orders. My feet dangle off the arm of the couch. I'm surprised and delighted at how cozy and intimate this feels. He starts handling my body – squeezing my breasts roughly, treating me as an object for his pleasure.

"Unbutton your jeans, slut. Let's see if you're already turned on." His fingers tease my desperately wet cunt. "You're always so wet."

"Yes, for you, Sir," I answer.

"I like that, it helps me save on lube," he comments. "How does it feel without underwear beneath your jeans?"

"Interesting, Sir."

He scowls. "Tell me more."

I scramble to answer, "The friction of my cunt against the denim is arousing."

He waits, expectantly.

"Sir," I blush. "It's arousing, Sir."

"You did a good job with your shirt," he compliments.

Before I can stop myself, I answer, "I did the best I could with such short notice, Sir."

His voice is stern. "You had plenty of notice. I didn't expect you to go shopping for an outfit to wear. I wouldn't want that unless I gave you money for it."

"I know, Sir."

"I'm serious about that."

I bite my tongue, but in my head I answer *Of course you're serious about it, Mr. Boundary-Pants. I do respect your boundaries, even if I don't agree with them.*

"While I eat my lunch," he glances at the burrito on the coffee table, "you're to go into the bedroom and make my bed. Announce that you've finished that task and then arrange yourself on the bed with your pants pulled down around your knees and your ass on display."

I'm reluctant to leave his side, but know I need to obey.

"Go, now." He interrupts my reverie. "You need to work on being more submissive, slut."

Embarrassed, I jump at his words. "Yes, Sir." In the bedroom I find clean sheets folded at the foot of the bed. I make the bed, pull the corners as taut as I can. *Does he expect hospital corners?* Hopefully the bed will get messed up anyway.

"I'm finished, Sir." I call to him, then remove my jeans and lay on my belly with my ass presented to him as requested.

As I wait for him to join me, I hear him pick up what sounds like my collar. A thrill ripples through me. He enters the bedroom. "Mmm, that's what I like to see – a whore ready for me." He checks my work. "Well done," he says, "you've apparently made a bed before."

He stands behind me to inspect my ass and cunt, spreads me wide with his fingers. Then he kneels beside me on the bed to fasten the collar around my neck. *As it should be*, I think to myself, in reaction to having collared myself last time we played. He uses his bare hand to spank me. I count each strike under my breath, even though he doesn't demand it. But once he passes 37, the number I expect (it's how old he turned last week), I give up on numbers. When he does finally stop he asks, "How many was that?"

All I can say is, "Fuck. I lost count, Sir."

His warm laughter soothes my fear about losing track. "Do you want more?"

I pause. My first instinct is to play at deference but that doesn't feel right. And I realize I do want more. "Yes please, Sir."

"Good answer," he replies, and starts in again. After the spankings he drips lube into the crack of my backside which I hope means he's going to fuck me. He slides a large plug into my ass instead. "How's that vibrating feature feel?" he asks.

"Strange," I reply, not used to things buzzing inside me.

He puts a dildo in my cunt too. I am stretched open and full. "Will those both stay put if you put your jeans back on?"

"I'm not sure, Sir." He decides to leave only the ass plug in place and tells me to pull up my pants.

"Come back into the front room," he says, grabbing the bottle of lube, "I'm going to fuck your tits." I follow him to the other room and kneel in front of him, hands behind my back. "Kiss my cock," he demands, looming over me. I lean forward and kiss the bulge through his jeans. He takes his time to undo his belt and slaps me lightly in the face with it before releasing his hard cock from his blue and red striped boxer briefs. (So much more fun than his usual plain white ones!)

With thin, coarse rope, he binds my arms behind my back, then sits back in the chair, and tells me to lean forward. He holds my tits together and slides his cock between them. I am kept slightly off balance in this position and I feel the rope pull at my wrists.

He seems frustrated and I can't tell why. Before I figure it out, he shakes his head. "I like you bound, but I'd rather you hold your tits around my cock." He thrusts his cock a few more times, then switches tactics.

"Do you want to suck my cock, slut?"

"Yes, Sir. Please let me suck your cock."

He reaches to grip my hair at the back of my neck, then pushes my face toward his erection. I don't have time to be nervous, after what felt like dismal failure at this task last time. I swallow him as deep as I can, force myself to push past the urge to gag.

"Good girl, stay right there." His praise helps me hold still as I attempt to breathe around him.

Just when I'm afraid I'll really choke, he slides out of my mouth and pushes me back up on my knees. I glance at his face to see him flushed. He's close to coming. He replaces my mouth with his hand, jerking himself off.

"I'm going to cum on your chest, whore." He barely has time to finish his sentence before my tits are covered in his cum. He flattens his hand against me and spreads the cum into a thin layer across my chest. "You'll leave this here until I give you permission to wash it off."

My face reacts with fear and arousal. *I'm going to work after this. I can't see clients smelling like sex. But how fucking hot is it to not have permission to wash this off?*

He interrupts my internal dialogue. "Lick this off my hand, bitch. Then clean my cock with your mouth." I rush to obey, delighted to be used in this way. When I finish, he reaches behind me to release my hands.

He scoots to the end of the couch where we started this scene. "Come up here and lie in my lap again." I'm shocked but I climb up where he wants me. "You have my permission to get yourself off, slut. And you'll thank me out loud as you cum."

I immediately shove my hand between my legs, fingers slipping in my sopping wet folds. My clit is hard and sensitive. His hand idly slaps my tits where his cum has dried into my skin. I'm flooded with sensory input and can't quite cum. I take a risk. "Sir, are you willing to fuck me with your hand while I get myself off? Please?"

He smiles. "Such a brave whore - and a greedy one." But he obliges me. Two fingers plunge into my cunt and I think this will put me over the edge. I let myself thrust against him as he taunts me. "Aren't you going to cum for me, slut? This is your chance."

But I can't. I have to ask him to stop because there's no way I'm going to orgasm. I'm spun out and exhausted. "Please stop, Sir. I'm done." He brings his hand to my mouth one last time. I lick him clean without being told.

"Good girl," he says with a smile. He lets me lay there with him for a few minutes while my nervous system recalibrates. I feel the clock ticking. This lunch hour is almost over.

"Sir?" I ask.

"What is it?"

I struggle over my words. "Well, Sir…As hot as it is to not wash this off my chest…" I can't look at him; embarrassment colors my cheeks. "I have to see clients after this."

He laughs out loud. "It's okay, you can wash it off. I don't expect you to go to work like that. Although that'd be hot."

"Yes, Sir," I agree. "It would. But I'll settle for rope marks that'll still be visible when I get to work." That gets another grin out of him.

He unbuckles my collar and tells me to go wash up and get dressed. I find a washcloth in the bathroom and wash my chest clean, then put my clothes back on. When I walk back into the living room, he is standing up, fully dressed too.

"I'll walk you to your car on my way back to the office," he says.

As I put my shoes on and gather my purse, I remember his birthday gift tucked inside it. I hand him a package wrapped in brown paper and tied with a bright orange piece of rope. He shakes his head at me with a smile on his face. "Happy birthday, Sir."

We leave the house together and when we reach my car he leans in for a hug. "Thank you, Sir, for planning such a creative scene. That was fun."

"Thank you. We make a good team."

As I get into my car and prepare to drive away, I watch him stride up the block in the sunshine toward his office.

Reflections for Sir:
It's exciting to never know what you have planned for us. Each scene has been unique, thanks to your creativity. Yes, we collaborate, but you do the lion's share of the work as the top. Great job with time management yesterday, it worked out so well!

What did you mean when you said I need to work on being more submissive?

Having my wrists bound created interesting sensations both while you manipulated the rope and also while servicing your cock. The rub of the rope on my hands and wrists was sensual. And going to work with rope-marks still visible was edgy and entertaining. I think I'll really enjoy having marks from other rope bondage we do in the future. I'm no longer averse to marks that can be covered by clothes.

You didn't give me much of a chance to suck your cock, but I felt more confident and relaxed. I was grateful for the positive feedback. Having you cum on my chest was sexy, and if I hadn't been so distracted by the worry about work after playing, I could have sunk into how delicious it was to have you spread your cum all over my tits and instruct me not to wash it off. I loved licking your hand clean and being ordered to clean your cock – such an incredibly submissive task.

It was frustrating that I couldn't cum when given the chance. It was a lot of pressure and I was over-stimulated (in delightful ways). I wrestled with myself about asking you to fuck my cunt, wondering if the request was out of line. But I figured I couldn't really go wrong if I asked politely. Even though I couldn't cum, it was so hot for you to praise, taunt, slap, and fuck me while I lay with my head in your lap. And I just had to give up on the orgasm – we didn't have all day!

I was anxious about not getting my instructions sooner. I wondered if that was an intentional mind-fuck or if you were just busy. When you said you'd been sick, I imagined that might have contributed. I also thought maybe you were working out the details of the scene.

Speaking of sick, I got the cold. I blame my daughter, not you. My brain's a little fuzzy as I write this.

I liked the service task of making your bed. Seeing the laundry basket full of clothes made me a bit wistful. I do enjoy folding your laundry.

Being on display for you is fun. I appreciate that you like what you see.

You strike an interesting mix of foreshadowing and surprise. Both are effective and tantalizing in their own way.

I noticed you praised me more during this scene than any other time we've played. Was that conscious and intentional? Was it because you went with a more casual vibe? Was my performance that noticeably improved?

Would you be willing to give me an idea of when we might see each other again and for what (lunch scene, longer scene after work, dominoes and chat)? I appreciate having something to anticipate, even if it's a bit in the future. I don't mean any pressure and I'm not anxious about it.

I hope you liked your birthday gift. *The Golden Compass* is one of my favorite books. And I couldn't resist the skein of rope as ribbon to tie off the package.

# SETTING IT ASIDE

Looking at Mr. Lucky's BDSM profile, I'm often intrigued by the photos he likes of women doing kinky, submissive things. Part of me responds with interest and curiosity; I enjoy the glimpse into what he finds attractive. But another part speaks in the voice of comparison. This is always a losing proposition. The women he's drawn to are smaller, more conventionally attractive, and sexier than me.

One photo he liked shows a woman dressed only in lime green, lace-trimmed panties and matching bra. She's not rail thin but her body seems taut and in shape. She is on her hands and knees, facing away from the camera, and the photo is taken from behind her. Balanced on her ass is a goblet of red wine, presumably belonging to the person she is serving. Mr. Lucky had me in a similar position when we played recently when I was his table. When I saw the photo he liked on the BDSM site, I conjured a mental image of myself in that pose and was flooded by negative, insulting thoughts about myself. I cut myself down with a quick and virulent intensity.

Driving to his place last week to play, I carried that image and the shame it evokes in my pockets. I worried it would get in the way of showing up with him, but I was determined to relax and enjoy the scene.

The thing I haven't been able to figure out is that once I am in his presence, especially once our scene starts, none of the shame or fear about my body or whether I am desirable is present. It all seems to leave my body and my consciousness the minute I submit to him. This amnesia is a relief, I just don't quite understand it.

With other lovers I'm usually hyper aware of what I don't like about my body. Matthew told me repeatedly how beautiful he found me, which helped, but there were still moments when I was aware of feeling shame about my body.

So is it about the act of submission? The night I met Mr. Lucky I was my typical fidgety self while we played word games – pulling at my shirt, shifting in my seat. But once we started scening, all that discomfort vanished. I attribute some of it to our opening ritual that grounds me in our dynamic. When I kneel before him and speak the words that signify my submission, I'm transported to a different presence. From that moment forward, each time we've played, I haven't given the size, shape, or functionality of my body a thought in any disparaging way. This reprieve from my self-hatred is one more reason I adore playing with him.

One other piece of this astounds me. Not only do I get this relief from body shame, but I'm able to be fully present in my body. I can feel the sensations and experience pleasure in my body exactly the way it is.

# MOVING BEYOND THE OBSESSION

Earlier tonight, I got antsy about hearing from Mr. Lucky. I plotted casual attempts to get him to respond to the writing he requested. The more I thought it over the more my anxiety spiked. Then I took a mental step back and realized I had so many other things to do tonight. There were questions to answer for an online interview project and claims to submit for work. I needed to call my sister about plans later in the week. I had writing to do from the process work I did this weekend on retreat with my women's group.

Yes, I would love to hear back from Mr. Lucky sooner than later, but I will eventually hear back from him. He's just one of the many things happening in my life right now. He might be the only game in town currently in terms of sex or play, but in the grand palette of my days, he is only one hue.

So I came home, put the kid to bed and set to work at my computer doing all the other things. I'm not anxious about Mr. Lucky in this moment. He crossed my mind many times today, but so did lots of other people I care about. More and more, he's just a dude.

*Sun, Nov 10, 2013 at 1:41 PM*
*thanks, i enjoyed your reflections.*

*this email is more cursory than i intended, but i'm afraid i
would never get done at the rate i'm going. the great is the
enemy of the good, as they say.*

*i enjoyed your perspectives in the scene recap, as well as the
alternating styles. i laughed at your positive reaction to my
striped underwear, and at the points where you revealed
what you were thinking in scene and i found that i had
properly guessed, or that I hadn't.*

*the eye contact in the opening ritual sure is intense.*

*saying you need to be more submissive was mind-fuck more
or less. but it's true in a general sense; there's always room
for improvement for everyone.*

*the couch interaction was a good way to connect, and i
could tell that it worked for you. my project is to find ways
to enjoy your submission that are actual sources of pleasure
for me, not things that i am driven to do by a sense of doing
it right or whatever. harder than i thought it was!*

*i think procrastination should get the lion's share of the
blame for when my instructions got to you.*

*and damn. i'll take the lion's share of the blame for you
catching the cold. sorry.*

*i've always enjoyed playing with anticipation and sexual*

*tension, but i haven't been thinking about it as a conscious plan with you. most interesting.*

*yes, praising you more was intentional. yes, it was about the casual vibe. and yes, your performance had improved.*

*having you lick up my cum was a challenge for me, due to the post-orgasm sex-drive-drop we've discussed. it's a switch from a dominance driven by physicality to one driven more cerebrally. it worked out nicely. anything with a mouth involved, you know...*

*that's too bad that you were frustrated, but you not coming is not a big deal from my perspective. it was still a hot sequence.*

*i like to think about exerting sexual dominance over longer periods of time and distance. the possibilities are fascinating.*

*i think we should try an evening session again. friday?*

Mon, Nov 11, 2013 at 8:00 AM
Ha! I wondered if that was happening. I considered suggesting you put down your metaphorical pencil and just send me what you had written already. It's not my place to rush you, but the thought made me smile.

I'm happy that you enjoyed the recap. It was unusually free and transparent writing. I had fun with it.

Without over-thinking it, I'd love a brief example of one guess you got right, and one you didn't. Indulge me?

When submitting, I forget that there's pressure for a top to do it right. I want you to find actual sources of pleasure while enjoying my submission. It makes me wonder if this is difficult just with me or with other subs too.

You don't get much of the blame for my getting sick. It's not like you kissed me or anything...

Conscious or not, the way you've played with anticipation each time has been fucking hot.

I couldn't tell it was a challenge for you in the moment. And yes, I know about you and mouths... I'm curious about your experience of dominance from both contexts.

My lack of orgasm isn't a big deal from your perspective? Somehow that's funny.

I feel like I am loosely in service to you from the minute I receive your instructions, especially once I am actively preparing myself to scene with you - shower, shave my legs, dress according to your instructions, and make sure I arrive on time. I'm game to explore this together over longer periods of time and distance, if you wish at some point.

Friday sounds great. I work until 6 pm and am free the rest of the evening.

# THE FIRST TIME...

The first time I talked about him in women's group I skirted so much of the truth there was hardly anything to say. Fear of judgment or being misunderstood kept me from speaking plainly. So I talked around it about my attraction, the ways we are similar, the synergy of our written correspondence.

The first time we met I was so nervous. What if the connection we'd established in writing didn't exist in person? What if he didn't want me once we met? What if my shyness created untenable awkwardness that destroyed our chance to play?

The first time I knelt before him I felt the power of our connection ignite in each of us. My fear dissolved in that instant, replaced by trust and the thrill of delicious unknown adventures to come. Through absolving myself of responsibility and control I surrendered to the gift of fully inhabiting my body. My only task was to follow his orders.

I was proud of pushing myself not only to write about Mr. Lucky but to also read it out loud at writing group. I often censor myself about my involvement in kink, and I just decided to give myself permission to read it. There's a level of safety built into the writing group structure that assumes everything we write is a work of fiction, not a story from our own life. This is another example of accepting that it's okay to tell the truth about my life, which includes the fact that I'm a sexual being who enjoys a specific kind of sex.

*Thu, Nov 14, 2013 at 12:01 PM*
*this all deserves an actual reply, but i'm struggling with communications right now.*

*friday is a go. 8 pm if that works.*

*only one instruction: bring your cock-sucking practice implement.*

# SCENE NUMBER FIVE
### November 15, 2013

I park across from his house precisely three minutes before I am expected. In the quiet car, I take several deep breaths to ground myself in my desire. I give myself permission to want this. At 7:59 p.m., with one minute to spare, I step out of the car and approach his blue bungalow. The click of my heels on the concrete keeps time with my rapid pulse. He greets me at the door with a warm hug and that smile of his that sizzles my heart. I pull away from his embrace to sit down on the couch and remove my boots. "Oh, you're all dolled up," he remarks, as my knee socks, black skirt and low-cut sleeveless shirt make their collective impression on him.

"I was left to my own devices; someone had to decide what I was going to wear," I say with a broad smile on my face. He laughs, knowing I prefer when his instructions for a scene dictate my attire. I set my boots near the front door and take a minute to acclimate to my surroundings. The fireplace hosts a rustling fire for heat and ambience. Three star-shaped paper lanterns cast a warm light above the couch. Vaguely recognizable music comes from a stereo in the far corner.

"Is there anything I need to know before we begin?" he inquires.

"I brought the toy, as instructed. Where shall I put it?" I ask, resisting the urge to call him Sir, since we aren't yet in role. With a smirk, he points to a low shelf behind me. Once I do, he catches my eye, and invites me to begin the scene.

He settles himself on the couch, watches as I kneel before him with my hands clasped behind my back. Our eyes meet. My voice crackles with desire as I recite my vow of submission, "While I am here, I am yours to use in any way you choose, Sir." The air between us electrifies. Reluctantly breaking eye contact, I punctuate my subservience with a kiss to his bare foot. My forehead rests on his foot as I wait for further instructions.

He grabs a fistful of my hair and tugs firmly. "I'm going to collar you, but first you have to earn it," he says. "You will kiss my feet, then work your way slowly up to my cock." He releases his grip on my hair and I set to work, tenderly kissing his feet and ankles. I nuzzle the rough texture of his Lucky Brand jeans as I trail kisses up his calves and thighs, alternating legs as I go. Tiny moans escape from me the closer I get to my destination. Reaching his crotch, I place my hands on his hips, and deliver several focused kisses to the bulge in his jeans. "Good job, slut. Now kiss your way back down to my feet. And don't forget to take your time." I do as I'm told, and when my lips graze his feet again, he orders me to stop.

Pulling my collar out of his pocket, he reaches down to slip it around my neck. A sound—half-sigh, half-whimper—spills from my lips. I hurry to move my hair out of the way as he fastens the buckle. He pulls on it gently, checking that it's secure, but not too tight. I don't even try to hide my pleasure at wearing it.

"You like that part," he notes, with a smile in his voice.

I nod, "Yes, Sir."

"Because it means you're owned," he continues.

"Because it means I'm yours, Sir."

My next task is to fetch an assortment of items from a nearby bookshelf, including a blindfold, leather cuffs, and a length of rope. I hand him each item before kneeling in front of him again. He leans forward to place the blindfold on me then tells me to turn around. I shift onto my hands and knees as he buckles one leather cuff onto each of my ankles. His hand travels slowly up the inside of my leg. "Good choice of tall socks. I like those," he comments, before slipping two fingers inside my panties to explore.

Gasping at his touch, I manage to say, "Thank you, Sir. I pay attention when you state a preference."

"That seems wise," he answers, removing his fingers from my now dripping cunt. "Get up on your knees again, facing the couch." I comply quickly. He reaches for my shirt, pulls it over my head, and adjusts the blindfold back into place. Adeptly unhooking my bra, he lifts it up without removing it entirely, leaving my breasts to hang freely. He grips and releases my flesh, and I feel the sting of his hand slapping first one breast then the other. He alternates back and forth, as I focus on my breathing to process the impact. "Take your bra off," he orders. "Let's see if one really can learn breast bondage by watching videos online."

Standing behind me, he reaches around my body to thread the thick, black rope under my heavy breasts. I lean into him, desperate to feel his body against mine. He steps back and I nearly lose my balance. Without a word he continues his task. As he manipulates the rope around my chest, I nuzzle my face against his arm. He breaks the contact. "You're going to find yourself in a mess of trouble if you don't stop improvising," he warns. I smile and force myself to refrain from playing with that fire. I'm tempted to discover what being in trouble with him feels like, but my job is obedience.

The harness lifts and separates my breasts, wrapping around my chest in a figure eight pattern. The rope stretches tight across my back and he brings one end around toward my face. "Open your mouth," he demands. He inserts the length of rope in my mouth and says, "Close." The process repeats on the other side. I open and shut my mouth as instructed. My teeth didn't know they craved something to bite down on, but the pressure is a focal point that tempers my longing for him. At his command, I release the rope ends into his hands. He ties off the harness and steps back to admire his work. "Yes, that will suffice," he says.

"Now, about that toy you brought…" He retrieves the dildo from the shelf where I'd set it. My breath catches in my throat, nervous energy clamors through my veins. "What have you been working on with this?"

My voice is hardly audible, drowned in the embarrassment of speaking these words. "Endurance, Sir, and depth."

"Excellent. Anything else?" He enjoys watching me blush.

"Noise, Sir - wet, slurping sounds…"

"Show me," he commands, placing the smooth, black, silicone cock in my hands before sitting down on the couch in front of me.

My face burns. My body pulses with desire. Grateful for the blindfold, so that I don't have to see him watching me, I bring the dildo to my lips. My tongue darts out to caress the tip of the toy as I warm up to the task. My mouth opens wide to swallow as much of the length as I can. I suck deeply. Pulling it back out inch by inch, I slurp the saliva in my mouth then slide the toy back toward my throat. His silent, hungry gaze surrounds me. He wants this and I am there to please him. I switch up my technique, take breaks as needed. To catch my breath, I lick up and down the length of the shaft before starting again. Finally, he interrupts me. "Well done, whore. Time to see how you do with the real thing."

Giving him head is an exercise in patience and humility. It is both challenge and reward. He has precise expectations for the performance of this task and he guides the process both physically and verbally. He's in complete control over every aspect of my movement – when I suck, lick or kiss, how deep I take him into my mouth, if I'm allowed a break. I whimper with anticipation as he unbuckles his belt and opens the buttons of his fly. "Are you ready to suck my cock?" he asks, pulling it free from the confines of his clothing.

I take a deep breath to relax my jaw. "Yes, Sir." Inching closer to him, I arrange myself between his legs. I lean forward to inhale his warm scent of sweat and desire. Before my lips caress his erection, he grabs my hair in his fist again.

"What are you?" he says.

"Your cock whore, Sir."

"Yes you are, aren't you?" he chuckles. "Start by kissing my balls."

His verbal commands are interspersed with praise. He calls me a good slut, admires my obvious desire to please him. As his submissive, I am in my element: collared, on my knees servicing his cock, flooded with devotion. He is clearly in no rush to cum, which I take as a sign that he enjoys my efforts. Offering me a welcome break, he tells me to stop, removes the blindfold, and invites me to rest my cheek on his thigh. I shift my weight off my knees, lean into him, and sigh contentedly. "Relax. Just rest." He strokes my hair as I calm my breath, savoring this closeness.

With a light tug at my hair he says, "Back to work, slut." I rise up to my knees and attend to his cock with renewed energy. With my mouth open wide I swallow the length of him deep into my throat. When I start to choke, I breathe through it without backing off. "That's right, stay there," he encourages, my neck held in place by his firm hand. Just as panic begins to seep into my consciousness, he lets up. His penis slides out of my mouth, and I gulp in air before wrapping my lips around the tip again. His hand grips the base of his shaft, jacking himself off as I noisily use my tongue against a mouthful of cock. "Suck, hard," he commands, and I feel him tense just before he cums. I know to hold his load in my open mouth, to wait for permission to swallow. After a minute that feels like ten, he says, "Go ahead." Relieved, I close my mouth and let the warm, salty fluid slide down my throat.

I collapse forward onto his lap. His hand rests on my head as we both take this chance to recover. After several minutes of peaceful silence he orders me to sit up. He inspects my breasts, notices their change in color from being bound. He pinches my nipples until I gasp from the intensity. "Let's get this harness off of you." He unties the knots in smooth, quick motions and my breasts flop against my body.

"May I use the bathroom, please, Sir?"

He nods. "Also," he says, "if you need water now is the time to get it. Or if you've taken up drinking, you can help yourself to some wine."

"I have a funny story for you about that, Sir," I respond, on my way through the bedroom to the bathroom. The clatter of the ankle cuffs against the hardwood floor startles me, and I walk the rest of the way on my tiptoes to quiet the sound.

When I return with a glass of water he says, "Why don't you sit on the floor and tell me your story." I explain that with my recent first taste of pear brandy a friend directed me to hold the liquor in my mouth as long as possible before I swallowed. "Ah. Always practicing…" he replies, his laughter as warm and intoxicating as the brandy had been. I swallow the last of my water and am told to return my cup to the kitchen. As a reflex, I glance at his wine glass, in case it needs to be topped off. It's full again which means I missed a chance to serve him. I flinch with disappointment.

Back in the living room, I take my place on my knees in front of him. "You have chores to do, bitch," he says. He nods at the basket of clean clothes next to me on the floor. "You will fold laundry while I get some writing done."

"Yes, Sir," I reply with a grin on my face. We both know this is one of my favorite service tasks. I fold his clothes with precision, create separate stacks for shirts, pants, and briefs. But it's his Lucky jeans that really delight me, ever since that first time I unbuttoned his jeans to find *Lucky You* sewn into the fly.

As I reach for the last shirt to fold, he stands up, grabs the basket and walks out of the room. He returns with another load of laundry and I brace myself, expecting him to dump the contents of the basket on my head. I am shocked when he places it at my side instead. This batch mostly contains bedding, so I ask, "Sir, is there a bed to make, or shall I fold the sheets?"

"No need to fold them, you'll make the bed with those sheets." I set the linens aside, fold the towels, and match the socks into pairs. Both loads of folded laundry fit into the basket. "Excellent work," he says, his eyes still focused on the screen of his laptop. "Go make the bed and return here when you finish."

I gather the bedding and head into the adjacent bedroom. As I make quick work of the bed, I let myself ponder what else he has planned for me tonight. *Why did he cuff my ankles? What does he intend?* I saunter back into the living room, aware of his eyes on me. Once again, I take my place on my knees with my hands clasped behind me. "That was fast. You're such a useful whore to have around."

"Thank you, Sir."

"Now, I want you to lie down at my feet while I work." I stretch out on the rug in front of him, my head resting on my folded arms. The room glows orange as the flickering firelight warms my half-naked body. I float in the marmalade of sensations: the weight of his foot on my bare back, the lingering sweetness of shared laughter, the sound of his fingers on the keyboard, the rough movements of his hands as he arranges my skirt to exact the precise view of me he desires, him sipping his wine. I am blissful and buoyant, anchored only by the scratchy nub of the rug beneath me, which smells faintly of cat hair and smoky embers. My mind wanders. *Why can't I always fold his laundry, lie at his feet while he writes, serve him wine, and be available to suck his cock? What the hell is wrong with that idea?*

He interrupts my reverie to ask, "Can you articulate the difference between the words supine and prone?"

I consider his question. "No, Sir. I know both words but can't differentiate them in the moment. I bet Google can." He scoffs at my response and continues writing. As I float back to the daydream of being owned by him more often, he uses his foot to hike up my skirt. His toes wriggle into my orange and purple polka-dotted panties to discover how wet I am for him. He toys with me as I sigh and moan at his touch. He rests his feet again on my back. Desire drips from me. My want for him is boundless.

"Get up, bitch. Go into the bedroom and take off your underwear. Stack the pillows at the foot of the bed and arrange yourself atop them, face down, ass up."

Before his command registers so I can heed it, he barks at me, "Go. Now."

I spring up and rush to obey. And then I wait.

The thud of his laptop closing startles me. He enters the room. "Hmm, sexy." He lifts my skirt up to expose my bare ass and a chill runs through me. One at a time, he fastens my ankle cuffs to bolts on the corners of the bed. He runs one hand up my leg, handling his property with rough authority. Without warning, he shoves two fingers inside my cunt.

"Mmm, yes…" I whisper, dissolving into his touch. He fucks me only enough to leave me wanting, then extracts his fingers and climbs onto the bed beside me. He knots a slender piece of rope around the center of the headboard and trails it toward me along the bed. "Bring your hands together above your head," he orders. I flatten my forearms against the mattress and arrange my hands as instructed. My wrists are bound together and secured to the headboard. I breathe in and exhale slowly, relaxing into this bondage.

He is slow and deliberate as he unbuckles his belt. It slides through the loops of his jeans with a soft whoosh. I tense, a mix of fear and anticipation. He's never used a belt on me before. One of his hands rakes through my hair and pulls it taut. My breath retracts and I hold it there. The first strike of his belt lands across my backside. I want to shrink away from the sting but I don't move. It takes all my concentration to remain still. Again and again his belt lashes against my body. It is almost unbearable, sharp and biting against the tender flesh of my inner thighs. No longer able to hold still, I struggle against the bonds holding me in place. He pauses. His flat palm skims across the welts rising up on my ass and legs. "How many strokes was that, whore?"

"Damn it," I mutter under my breath. This is a standing joke between us. He knows the impact interrupts my ability to count. "I have no fucking idea...Sir."

"Well, then, we'll just have to start again." This time I will myself to keep track. He strikes me ten more times. I breathe through the pain and count each one aloud with tears in my eyes. "Good girl," he praises. He lets go of my hair and climbs down off the bed. My heart begins to slow its racing. The next sound I hear is a squirt of lube before I feel him behind me. He shoves the toy cock inside me. He taunts me, pulls it out of my cunt slowly, listening to me moan with need. After a few more thrusts, he leaves me vacant and hungry. The room goes dark when he switches off the lamp. He throws a heavy, warm blanket over my body. "I'll be back when I'm ready to use you again, whore." I hear the door shut behind him as he leaves the room.

I vacillate between impatience and contentment as I wait. And wait. And wait. I hear only the sound of my own breath. I feel the tug of the cuffs at my ankles, a slight ache creeps into my shoulder from holding this position. *When will he come back? How will he use me? Please let him fuck me more. Will this be the scene when he finally kisses me?* Only once do I panic — as I remember the fire burning in the fireplace. *If the house caught fire, would he get to me in time to release me from the bondage?* I shake away the thought. More waiting. My internal clock says it's been fifteen minutes but it could have been seven, or thirty. Anticipation can't tell time.

Finally, the doorknob turns and he enters the room. "How are you doing in here, slut?" he asks. "What are you thinking about?"

My cunt contracts with desire at the sound of his voice. "Getting fucked by you, Sir."

He yanks the blanket off of me. "Where do you want my cock?"

I know no deference in this moment. "Cunt, Sir. I want you to fuck my cunt."

"Let me hear you beg for it, slut."

The words tumble from my mouth. "Please, Sir, fuck my cunt. Use me like the slut I am for you. Slam your hard cock all the way inside me. I need it, Sir. Please, Sir, I need you to fuck me. Please, Sir, now, Sir..." Through my litany, I don't hear him remove his jeans and boxer briefs. I don't notice him rip open the condom wrapper and slide it down his shaft. He halts my begging with his hands on my hips, pulls me back onto his hard cock. Each thrust is an answer to my longing. The sway and push of my hips meet his over and over. I am loud - moans, gasps, and unintelligible bliss pouring from me unabashedly.

"That's sexy," he growls. With those words I am broken open, riding the crest of this ecstasy. He fucks me for what feels like hours, first with his cock, then his fingers, then the dildo. I grip the rope between my hands, steady myself with it as he uses me with abandon. When he stops, briefly, my voice protests in a pout against my will. "Don't cry," he jokes. He unhooks my ankles from the bed frame, buckling the cuffs to each other instead. "You'll be tied up again."

I laugh and ask, "Is that a promise, Sir?"

"Oh it's never a promise. No promises." He pushes the dildo back inside me and climbs up behind me on the bed. One of his hands reaches above my head, pressing down on my hands. His other hand is in my hair. He pushes my face into the mattress. All the while he fucks me with the toy cock, driving it into me with his thigh. I writhe against him. He trades out the toy for his fingers, straddles my lower back, and continues fucking me.

"That's all for you," he says, pulling his fingers from my sloppy cunt. He stretches himself out on top of me, his chest pressed against my back, the weight of him strikingly soothing. All too soon he begins to shift, as if to separate from me.

"No!" I nearly shout at him in fiery red fear, "Don't go."

"Hang on," he replies, matching my tenor and sounding slightly annoyed, "I'll be back." He unbuckles my ankle cuffs from each other and settles right back down on top of me. The force of him centers me. He wraps his arms around me, holding us in place. My breath slows as

I process the remains of the intensity. There aren't tears but there could have been; midnight blue sadness streams out of my pores, rendering me whole again. His stubble grazes my cheek. I am safe. I am grounded. I am his. In this moment we are one.

He starts to shift again and reaches to untie the knots that hold my wrists. I let him go without fussing only because he lures me under the covers to cuddle. Still coming down from the scene, I lie in his arms with my head nestled against his shoulder. We compare notes about our favorite moments from the evening, laugh at the synergy of our connection. Before I can mention how I expected him to toss the laundry over my head, he tells me that he almost did, but changed his mind at the last minute. When I rave about being bound while he fucked me, he smiles. "Bound with the rope you gave me?" I confirm that this detail was not lost on me. I ask whether my cock-sucking has improved, and he affirms that he has no complaints. We both express how hot the verbal exchanges were, from the scene-opening ritual to the begging and all the audible feedback throughout.

Emboldened by the intimacy of the moment, I attempt to ask him about kissing. In my nervousness, I start by quoting back to him what he told me about not kissing his submissives at first because it's so intimate. He teases me, "Were you going to put that in the form of a question?"

"I'm working on it," I answer. "It's just that your lips have never touched any part of my body and…" I trail off, afraid I've said too much.

"Is that true?" he counters.

"Without a doubt," I assert. He says he is still wary of it. I'm disappointed but not surprised. And really, with everything else we get to do together, I can forgo kissing.

Another hour passes as we lie there talking. He tells me about the awful day he had, how everything that could go wrong had, which made him fear that our scene would somehow fail. We rejoice together over how well it played out. I explain why I've been so emotionally raw lately and how cathartic it was to feel the full weight of him on top of me, holding me down. As the clock ticks past midnight we consider calling it a night. Just as we start to untangle our limbs from one another, he leans over and plants a delicate kiss on my forehead. I almost melt from the sweetness.

I find the pieces of my outfit that were shed throughout the evening and get myself dressed. He tends to the almost burned out fire. At the threshold of the front door, I fold myself into his arms and rest my head on his chest one last time before he sends me home, exhausted but satiated.

# EMOTIONAL SEDIMENT

This is the piece I wrote for this week's 33-word challenge:

*After weeks of clamoring for contact, this influx of intimacy soothes. Steeping in gratitude, I notice longing, both companion and counterpoint to satiety, threatening to wrestle me once again into the tumultuous tide.*

I'm still coming down from the delicious influx of intimacy over the weekend. The see-saw of gratitude and longing over the last several days has occupied most of my available brain and heart space.

I'm itching to write Mr. Lucky and share something I wrote at writing group last night. Summer asked why I want to send it to him; am I seeking his approval? My answer circles back to the word connection. Part of my desire to reach out to him is because of the emotional intensity we created together. We were so connected on Friday night, during and after the scene…and now there's just a vast nothingness.

I probably do want his approval. And yet I knew when I walked out of his house that night that we both felt the connection. This distance and lack of contact breeds the fear that something is awry.

He told me in no uncertain terms that he is struggling with correspondence right now. That isn't about me. He's traveling this week and next. He said there'll be time to see me at least a couple of times before traveling again in December.

I believe if I really needed some sort of contact from him, and I asked clearly and respectfully, he would reach back. My task is to manage my own emotions and figure out if there's something that I need from him, or if I can tend to my emotionality in therapy, at women's group, in writing, or all of the above.

# THIS IS WHY I GO TO THERAPY

Mr. Lucky and I have a little joke going about something he said in-scene that carries intense erotic pull for me: *You are not allowed to disguise any aspect of your arousal in my presence.* He calls it my 'climactic line' and likes to tease me about it. The other night after we played, Mr. Lucky quipped that I really need a bumper sticker of it. I replied, "yeah or a t-shirt or something."

He asked why it affects me so strongly. I explained that it ties into my fear of being too much and that I've had negative feedback from previous lovers about being loud during sex.

In therapy today, I told Gayle about it. She looked at me with tears in her eyes and asked, "Do you grasp the emotional significance of that sentiment for someone who has been made to hide her whole life?" I felt her words land in my chest as tears sprung to my own eyes.

"No," I told her, "I hadn't recognized that. Wow, you're right! I've been forced to hide the truth about myself, disguise my unique identity, stifle my voice, despise my body, and deny my desire and emotions. In my family and then in adult relationships, I have always been in hiding. For him to forbid it, is so powerful." Gayle pointed out that he's essentially saying: *I want all of you. I want to see you, hear you, know you. I want it all.*

She talked about how I'm required to disarm myself in order to engage with Mr. Lucky. I've told her how he's attuned to me, sharing examples from our scene the other night. She also referenced the sharpness of his touch. When she said the word sharp, the first image I got was of him slapping my face.

I explained to Gayle that I'd always been curious about being slapped and that playing with Mr. Lucky was the first time it happened. And I like it. It's evocative for me in a way I can't quite articulate. Gayle proposed that being slapped in the face is more personal than something like spanking. I agreed with her and then squealed with glee and relief that I can talk about all this and that she gets it.

At women's group tonight, explaining how much I've hidden myself away throughout my life, I also realized the effect of being on display and completely under Mr. Lucky's direction. I have no choice but to be seen and heard. It's vulnerable and edgy, especially when I'm blindfolded like the other night and my only option is to focus on my own experience.

Processing and exploring these details of our scenes may seem like obsession, but it isn't. This is how I find my way back to myself through powerful, attuned, physical, emotional, intellectual, and sexual presence – my own, and his, and the interplay between us. It's emotional integration and growth.

# RUNNING THOUGHTS

I am not too much. I am not too much. I am not too much. I am not too much.

Continue on repeat until intersected by running thought #2 I will NOT text Mr. Lucky to wish him Happy Thanksgiving. I will NOT text Mr. Lucky to wish him Happy Thanksgiving. I will NOT text Mr. Lucky to wish him Happy Thanksgiving. I will NOT text Mr. Lucky to wish him Happy Thanksgiving.

Thought #2 is self-explanatory. I am not too much relates to my fear of annoying him with the reflections from our last scene, but is also affected by spending the afternoon with my family. At family events, I'm suspended between the twin fears of being not enough or too much, ping-ponging endlessly. I generally show up excited to see everyone and then feel lonely because the connections fall short of what nourishes me.

Part of the solution is to lower my expectations to match my family's inclinations and abilities. The other part is to share more of my authentic self at every opportunity, to tell as much of the truth as I am willing to in any moment.

# TRIFECTA – WEEK #96

Floating under his star, my own compass willingly relinquished, his passion guided us. Riding on currents conjured within the weather pattern of his desire, the tides rose and receded as we sailed together.

# SUGGESTION BOX

True to my word, I haven't sent you a single text – ever really (just that one incident with the window blinds, but that was warranted!). It's especially difficult not to text you this week. Here are some of the texts I've drafted in my head, but haven't sent.

1) Hey, how was your trip? Did you survive SoCal?

2) I won one of the weekly Trifecta challenges!

3) Have you left for your Thanksgiving trip yet? Will you see both parents? Will your sister be there? Hope it's great.

4) Wow – I tied for 2nd in the next writing challenge! I'm on a roll! Woo-hoo!

5) You are going to respond to my last email novella, right?

6) Remind me again, please, exactly why you struggle so much with correspondence?

7) I have creative ideas about possible scene activities. Do you have a suggestion box?

8) I tasted five different kinds of alcohol on Thanksgiving. It was a fun experiment. This relates to #7.

9) I miss you and wish you were in town for my potluck this weekend.

10) I haven't asked about your painting in a while. How's it going? You were going to work on some new commissions – did that happen? How'd it go?

11) I heard Tom Petty on the radio again today. I listen to my own music so much, I forget to let the radio oracle bring me what it will. It often delivers a bit of Tom, which makes me smile and think of you. I've decided that along with "Into the Great Wide Open" our song is "You and I Will Meet Again." It soothes me when I'm antsy about seeing you.

12) Seriously, no response to my email yet? I know you're traveling, and struggle with emails. But really? A simple, fly-by I read this (yes all of it!) and liked it. Talk soon isn't possible?

13) I'm going to a sex-toy party tonight for a friend's 40th birthday. Any directions about what to purchase? ;)

Any of these could have been texted to you this week. Your quiet really stresses me out. It shouldn't, we're on firm ground. But it does. I've always sucked at patience anyway. Patience is like the middle name my parents planned for me but changed their minds once they laid eyes on tiny me, five weeks earlier than expected.

# TAKING RISKS

I've been taking risks by sharing my authentic self and using my voice in places where I historically wouldn't. The more I do this, the easier it gets.

At writing group, it's definitely less scary than it was at first to write what I write and share it. It's interesting what feels edgy there and what doesn't. When I write about tragedy, grief, or sorrow at writing group, it feels vulnerable but in an acceptable way. Lots of the women there write about similar themes so even though it gets intense, everyone can relate.

When I write about kink and my relationship with Mr. Lucky, I fear folks won't connect with it. It's uncomfortable. Twice now in the middle of a timed write at group, I've had to acknowledge my fear as I'm writing in order to continue with the prompt and be able to read it. It helps to just keep my pen moving by writing the words *I am afraid to write this here, but also afraid to not have anything to read* or *keep writing, it's okay.* I want to just go where my writing takes me, without edit, without worrying about perception. Of course, there are limits to what I will expose there. But they are fewer and less stringent than before.

Breaking through the barrier in women's group came partly from being myself with my friends on the retreat and honestly describing my relationship with Mr. Lucky.

# FRUSTRATED

When am I going to find someone who reciprocates my interest? When will I find someone who has time in his life and room in his heart to be with me? When am I going to find someone who can be a part of my daily life? When am I going to find someone who I can introduce to my family and friends as my boyfriend?

Argh! I hate this. I hate waiting. I hate trying to be patient. I hate putting myself out there on stupid dating sites, trying to get someone interested in me. I hate feeling invisible in the connections I do have. I can hardly talk about Mr. Lucky with anyone in my life. Okay that isn't true. I don't talk with my family about him, but nearly everyone else important to me knows about him and at least something about the nature of our relationship.

Driving home I blasted *Synchronicity* by the Police as loud as I could tolerate. I felt so much despair and anger and hurt. Am I really this broken? Am I so messed up that I play out my desperate need for connection in every relationship? Will it ever change? Or I am stuck this way, destined to reach for things that aren't offered to me freely?

It feels so fucking hopeless sometimes, seeking a partner who wants to be with me. I don't want to be alone. I'm tired of being with people who don't reciprocate my desire, but I'm not ready to be done with Mr. Lucky.

# HOLDING SPACE

My personality contains an amalgamation of my overactive planning brain, my general optimism, and my willingness to acquiesce to what works best for the other person involved in any situation. This isn't necessarily an asset to me.

I am unofficially holding space open in my schedule for when I might get to see Mr. Lucky over the next two weeks. It's ridiculous since I don't know when I'll hear from him or what he'll offer for getting together. But I'm extra aware of my schedule.

When my last client of the evening cancelled for this Wednesday night it felt auspicious because sometimes Mr. Lucky and I play on Wednesday and then we could start earlier. When a friend asked to stay with me two nights next week, I was clear that one of those nights I might have plans with Mr. Lucky.

I want to cover all my bases for when he suggests a time. Because he will, when he writes back, which he will.

He is perfectly aware that it's his turn to contact me. I am trying to chill out and give him some space. There was a lot to digest from my reflections. Not too much, I hope, but plenty.

# WRITING GROUP

I've been anxious and frustrated all day, on edge, waiting and waiting. Will relief arrive today in the form of a reply from him? I fiddle with words in my head, reach for a combination that hits the jackpot – a way to check in with him without wrecking the game. I try to dig within me to the calm centered clarity that trusts our connection and honors his integrity. That deeper wisdom eludes me in favor of high-pitched, nervous irritability.

I force myself to notice small gifts of the day – beautiful cloud patterns overhead, the sweetness of my daughter's hand in mine. I collect bits of joy from any available avenue while the waiting idles in the back of my mind. Friends make me laugh with their texts and social media posts, they share in my amusement at the kiddo's musical commentary.

And the waiting refuses to wane. It ticks, it tocks, relentless.

Our next writing prompt is to explore darkness and then shift into light…

Grief takes root in the body, nestling into marrow and muscle, knitting itself into skin, traveling through veins like emotional tributaries. To imagine metabolizing grief is to evoke hope, it implies movement, hints at grieving as a process in motion, not stuck or stagnant, not stifled. Letting oneself gurgle around moments of grief the way our bodies process the onslaught of a Thanksgiving meal.

Metabolism calls upon so many systems in our bodies, shifting our core temperature, our mood, our energy level. Grief does the same thing – numbing us out in frigid cold or raising our temperature until we break a sweat. We have to find a way to trust the darkness not as the end point of the journey, but a passage in the middle.

*You stopped writing because you're thinking about Mr. Lucky again. Can you set it aside to stay present here? Try, really try. Yes, a brief email just arrived from him in the middle of writing group. Put it aside.*

My constitution will never be the same after the losses I've endured. The fabric of my being is altered, irrevocably.

*I wouldn't long for his written self this much if I had not connected with it so strongly. Grr. Stop with him already!*

Losing the threads, can't focus. Just keep writing. Turn toward the light. Learning to recognize the ways in which my grief is healing blah blah blah.

*Argh, seriously? Fine, write about him.*

*I want more of you. What did you think of my reflections? What made you smile? Where did you cringe or groan? Did any of my positive feedback sink in? Does it matter to you? Do I matter to you, is the more pertinent question. Yes, a voice within me asserts. But she is not very loud or convincing.*

*I will read his message twenty times over. I will pine for more communication from him. His sparsely worded reply will offer slight reassurance, but it will not suffice. I will want more and more of him. Will that part ever end?*

Sometimes the beckoning light is muted, streamed through textured curtains, creating shadow patterns across the floor. Other times it casts a radiant glow over everything around you, bold, warm, and bright, unfiltered. Light and darkness wrestle for balance, chiaroscuro. Healing occurs through the doorways of contrast, on circuitous paths that lead from dark to light and back again.

Sometimes reaching for the light is scary. What if we lose again? What if the risk of connection and potential loss is worse than the loneliness of grieving? What if we open ourselves to love again and still remain alone? What then?


*Tue, Dec 3, 2013 at 6:45 PM*
*thanks. good stuff. the marmalade of sensations*

*i'm just back from the heartland and trying to get back into my groove, and this is too much for me to deal with processing right now, but i appreciate your downloads.*

*are you free next wednesday evening, 12/11?*

# REMINDERS

I texted Calvin yesterday: OMG I am so fucking anxious right now waiting to hear from Mr. Lucky. Old story, I know, but I'm in it again. His response was awesome. Why don't you dry off before you get pruned skin? With his perfect, shorthand reminder I felt seen and validated.

I'm disappointed that Mr. Lucky won't respond to the content of my reflections. It's difficult that what I wrote is too much for him to process. Summer says that's about him and his bandwidth, not about me. I really want to believe her but I'm not quite there.

Sometimes I worry about my need for an audience, someone to witness my experiences and my writing about them. And then I think about my history of not being acknowledged, respected, heard, or understood in my family. Is it any wonder that I need an audience? How could I not?

Wed, Dec 4, 2013 at 11:09 PM
Welcome back from the heartland! I hope your trip and holiday went well.

Thank you for reading my reflections. I appreciate knowing it is too much for you to deal with right now. I am free Wednesday, 12/11 from 8 pm on. Shall I plan on seeing you that evening?

# INTERSECTION

My relationship with Mr. Lucky exists at the intersection of my fears about being too much and not enough, of not being wanted, of having love, attention, and affection and then losing it again.

Summer says I talk about Mr. Lucky as if he's doing me a favor by playing with me. She insists that I'm not a charity case. I agree, mostly (sort of). And I comprehend that if he didn't want to play with me, he wouldn't. He isn't the sort to act from a sense of obligation or pity. He craves the release and enjoys our dynamic too. I meet his needs. I serve him well. He has fun and gets off. And if any of that changed for him, he would stop.

I stumbled in response to his email – it felt tricky to acknowledge that it was too much for him to process without apologizing for putting it all out there. And I wanted to say that I'm free Wednesday, but it wasn't clear what he was proposing. It felt safe to assume we would scene, but I didn't want to ask the question and belie my fear that he'll start another indefinite hiatus.

Those 29 hours until I replied were a lovely reprieve from the anxiety of waiting for his response. I held on to the fact that even if he won't respond to the content of my email, he wants to see me.

I'm afraid he's going to press pause again and I might scream. I need to ask for something tangible in the interim, something he's likely willing and able to deliver. Maybe a brief phone check in if we aren't going to see each other for more than three weeks?

*Mon, Dec 9, 2013 at 9:10 PM*
*Yes, if you are still free. Sorry about the lack of confirmation.*

Mon, Dec 9, 2013 at 9:31 PM
I am still free and have been holding the time open.
I guessed you might confirm by sending me instructions.

*Tue, Dec 10, 2013 at 8:00 PM*
*Good guess. I did at one point plan to do so.*

*Wear a coat, a skirt, and a shirt you can pull your tits out of. Nothing else.*
*Bring along the same toy cock as last time.*
*Pull out your tits before you put on your coat.*
*Get in your car and insert the toy deep in your cunt.*
*Drive to my house like this. Arrive at 8 pm.*
*Take out the toy.*
*Come to the front door, knock, and wait a few seconds.*
*Come inside, take off your coat, and put down your things.*
*Kneel in front of me and reinsert the fake cock in your cunt.*
*Begin the ritual.*

# TRIFECTA - WEEK #107

Anxious anticipation abounds, questions and uncertainties course aggressively through my veins. Our eyes meet, exchanging paragraphs of emotion in wordless greeting. Bodily tension subsides, my tight muscles melt, leaving me supple, present, open.

# SCENE NUMBER SIX
### December 11, 2013

My last client session ends just before 7 p.m., which leaves me an hour to prepare myself and arrive at Mr. Lucky's on time for our scene. I snack on cheese and crackers while putting away client files and read his instructions one more time. In the bathroom I splash water on my face, run my fingers through my hair. *Will he notice my new blonde highlights?*

Back in my office I remove the jeans and sweater I wore for work. I unfasten my bra and slip it off; panties too. The only shirt that meets his requirements is the same bright pink, low-cut t-shirt I wore once before. I pair it with a simple black skirt and am as dressed as he will allow. Wrapping my warm black pea-coat around me helps me feel less exposed. I still feel conspicuous as I lock up and walk through the deserted building to the empty parking lot.

In my car I pull the black silicone dildo out of my bag, drizzle a bit of lube on the tip and spread my legs to slide it inside me. Once it's secured, I buckle my seatbelt and head to his house, ten minutes away. I'm squirmy and uncomfortable but also aroused. Early as usual, I park half a block away and silence the engine. I reach between my legs to tease myself with the cock. *He didn't tell me not to enjoy it*, I reason. When it's time to go in I remove the toy, wrap it in a dark green handkerchief, and drop it into my purse.

Swallowing around my nervous energy, I knock at the door of the house, then let myself in as instructed. I sneak a glance as I cross the room to set my things down. I startle at the sight of him; even dressed in a t-shirt and flannel pajama pants he is sexy. He barely looks up from his book while I hang my coat and slip off my shoes. He ignores me until I present myself on my knees before him.

He smirks as I reinsert the toy into my cunt, then orders me to recite my ritual opening line. "While I am here I am yours to use in any way you choose, Sir." I bend to kiss his foot and wait. He reaches behind me to fuck me roughly with the toy, then removes it in one swift motion. The abrupt emptiness is excruciating; I want to whimper but don't.

"You have work to do, slut." He points out two cases of wine on the floor beside me. "Take each bottle out of the box, sort them by variety of wine, and gather all the packing peanuts into this large plastic bag." I nod. He steps close behind me to buckle my collar around my neck. A satisfied sigh escapes me as I feel the smooth leather against my skin. "When you're finished, you'll open a bottle of red wine and fill my glass."

*Fuck, is there a corkscrew nearby? I've never opened a bottle of wine, what if I can't do it?* My panic is mild, I hope he doesn't notice. I mostly don't drink, I've never opened a bottle of wine. He knows this and his mind-fuck is not accidental. "Scoot over, closer to the table," he commands. When I do, he wraps a leash around the nearest table leg then clips the end of it to the ring of my collar. The leash impedes my movement, which of course is the point. "Just to make sure you don't go anywhere," he jokes.

I set about my task, being careful but not as fastidious as I could be. He returns to reading. I feel his eyes on me intermittently as I work. When I'm nearly finished, I knock over a group of wine bottles. My breath stills until I'm certain none of them broke. Setting them back upright, I note that the red wine bottles have screw-tops, not corks. *Phew! I won't have to test my agility with the corkscrew!* I open a bottle of red and fill the small beaker he's using as a glass. After one more scan of the area, I let him know my task is complete.

His inspection uncovers a packing peanut and some other stray bits of debris on the ground. "This is the sort of thing I was hoping to avoid," he says, holding up the errant styrofoam. He lifts the hem of my skirt and spanks my bare ass several times. My body tenses. I shift slightly away from his hand. There isn't anywhere for me to go; I'm still bound to the table leg. "Hold still, slut," he growls. And I do through four more swats.

He unhooks the leash from the ring of my collar and orders me to stand. "Next you'll clean the bathroom. Wipe down the sink and tub. There are cleaning supplies in there already. When you finish, run a hot shower. Take off your clothes and kneel on the bathmat until I come in."

I cross the room and set to work. *Did he tell me to clean the toilet too? I don't think so. Damn, what if he did?* I compromise with myself and give the exterior of the toilet a quick wipe after finishing the tub and sink. Water on. Clothes off. Kneel.

After only a minute I hear him approach. He scans the small bathroom. "Good work." His praise paints a delicate blush across my cheeks. His fingers brush the back of my neck as he unbuckles my collar. He reaches over me to test the water temperature, adjusts it hotter. "Get into the tub and kneel facing the fixtures." I scurry to obey his command, acclimating to the warm shower as I wait for him to undress and join me. I've never seen him fully naked. My desire for him spikes as he steps into the spray, his hard cock directly in front of my eager mouth. I long to suck it but wouldn't dare without permission. My hunger for him is palpable.

"Kiss my balls, slut," he demands. "No cock." Water runs over my face and into my mouth as I lean in to kiss his balls. It's challenging and the struggle is hot. I broadcast my pleasure with loud smacking noises and low moans as I lick and kiss his balls, reluctantly avoiding his cock. His hand in my hair tugging me backward interrupts my joyful reverie.

"Stand up and trade me places," he says. This isn't simple in his small tub. I stand up and we hold onto each other to slowly rotate until I am closer to the running water. Suctioned onto the wall beneath the shower head is my black dildo. "You wanted a cock to suck, didn't you, whore?"

"Yes, Sir," I answer, amused and surprised.

"Suck that one while I fuck you with mine." I'm flushed from the heat of the shower and faint with desire. I bend forward from the waist to blow the dildo as I feel his hard cock against the edge of my ass. Just as I begin to push back toward him he stops. My whimper is drowned out by the noise of the shower. "Stand up, turn the water off." Confused and disappointed, I do as I'm told. "Step out of the shower and dry yourself off with the blue towel."

I climb out and fumble for the towel to dry myself, suddenly awkward in my nakedness and confusion. He joins me on the bathmat, still dripping. "You may use that towel to dry me off," he says. My nervousness evaporates in a rush of excitement at this tender way to display my devotion. Starting with his chest, I carefully attend to his body. We're rarely face to face, and truly, we aren't now either, we're more like face to chest. I stretch onto my tiptoes to reach his thick, dark, curly hair. He turns around for me to dry the broad expanse of his back. This is the most intimate act of service he's ever allowed me to perform for him. I want to draw it out for a long time, but I feel rushed so I don't linger. When I finish, he picks up my collar from the edge of the sink where he'd set it, and fastens it back into place at my neck. I grin.

I still have no idea why he stopped short of fucking me, but I know better than to ask. "Follow me back to the living room and refill my wine glass, then kneel at my feet." His voice is on edge; he sounds frustrated. I hand him his beaker of wine and kneel in my spot. When I realize my nose is running, I ask, "Sir, may I please get a tissue to blow my nose?" He grants permission. I stand up, walk to the bathroom, and take care of it, returning with extra tissues in case I need them.

"Time to show me what a cock whore you are," he commands, pulling his dick out of his pants as I drop to my knees again. "You are not to look anywhere else but at the cock you're worshipping." I nod but notice my nose start to drip again. *Fuck, not again already, I can't suck cock with a runny nose!*

"Sir, I need to blow my nose again." I'm already shifting in the direction of the table with the extra tissues. He leans forward and grabs my shoulder to stop me in my tracks.

I turn back around to face him; he's glaring at me, angry. "You ask permission before you move," he snarls at me. "I don't care if you have to blow your nose, this is your focus, slut." I'm humiliated but it turns me on. I like him mean.

"Yes, Sir. I'm sorry, Sir."

"Go ahead, but come right back." I scramble to the table on my knees, wipe my nose, and toss the tissue in the trash. Back in my place I wait for permission to begin. Without warning, he slaps me across the face. It startles me. The sharp sting and loud smack of his palm against my cheek gets me hot all over again. He slaps me six times, three on each cheek. I feel chastised and aroused.

"Now, bitch, get busy." I take his cock in my mouth, push myself to swallow it deep into my throat. I try to obey the eye contact restriction. After his sharp disciplinary tone, and the harsh slapping, I want to seek reassurance by looking him in the eye. But this isn't the time to push limits. I sneak tiny glimpses when I think he isn't paying attention.

He controls the pace of the blow job, instructs me every step of the way. No matter how much practice he offers me at giving head, I still don't comprehend how this process works for him. *Is it tedious to coach me or is that part of the fun? Would he rather just focus on his reading and not constantly monitor and teach me? Would he rather it not take so long to orgasm? But he controls the pace so this must be what he wants.*

His commands slow as he approaches orgasm. I feel his body go taut and his hand grips the back of my hair as his load erupts into my mouth. I force myself not to swallow. *Not until he gives you permission, don't fuck this up!* He pulls his cock out of my mouth and I struggle not to spill the mouthful of cum. "Open your mouth, bitch. Show me you didn't swallow yet."

I carefully open my mouth for his inspection. "Good girl. Go ahead and swallow." Relief washes down my throat – I didn't spill any, I didn't swallow too soon. I'm proud that I've done just what he expects. He pulls me to him, lets me snuggle my head onto his lap as we both catch our breath. He idly plays with my hair, stroking it gently.

"Thank you, Sir," I say, tentatively breaking the silence. "That was fun."

He smiles. "You're welcome, slut. And you're right, it was fun." We transition into debriefing the scene, sharing insights and moments from the evening. "This was the most excited I've been about a scene," he says. "Not nervous…"

"Nervous?" I echo.

"Yeah, about doing a good job," he answers. I react with a facial expression and tiny little *aw* sound. "It matters to me," he replies.

"I know it does," I reassure him. "You always do a good job."

He ignores my comment and instead answers, "Mostly I was just thinking, *I'm going to get my cock sucked tonight!*" I grin in response.

"I especially liked the face slapping tonight," I say, already reminiscing.

"Yes, it was harder than before too, like you said you wanted."

"It felt so good! I don't know what it is about that sensation but it feels amazing."

He laughs, agreeing with me. "You have a really strong neck," he continues. "Sometimes I can hardly move it when I want to." He reaches to demonstrate, pulling my hair to move my neck. "It's a lion thing."

*It's a lion thing?! What the hell?!* Just when I think he's aloof and not paying attention, he invokes my affinity for lions in this surprisingly attuned way.

"Can I ask you something?" I venture, carefully.

"Sure, what's up?"

"Why didn't you fuck me in the shower?"

"Technical difficulties – the lube washed off and I was worried about fucking your ass with no lube."

I nod. "That makes sense, thank you for clarifying."

Tonight is the only time we've played when there wasn't talk of next time. On the one hand, I appreciate it, because it would devastate me if he intimated that there'd be a next time and there wasn't. With so much positive momentum from this scene and ideas of other things to try, I definitely hope that there's a next time.

We sit on the couch, me snuggled into his warm body. Already on edge, I tiptoe into asking about his primary partner coming home. "What does she know about me?"

"She knows you exist but we haven't talked in detail, largely because of the distance and communication gap while she's been overseas."

"How will it affect our interactions when she's back?"

"She and I will need to have several long conversations and see where things stand. This will be the last time we play for a while…and I don't know what a while means."

Projecting the most casual calm I can muster, I ask, "Maybe not the last time ever, though?"

"Maybe not," he says. "I don't know for sure. We've had a good run…"

I untangle myself from his side and sit as far away from him on the love seat as I can. My voice dissolves in blistering panic and rage. He continues speaking, "I don't want to make any promises when I don't know how things will settle once she's home."

He promises to stay in better touch via email, without me asking for that. And he explains what happens for him with correspondence. "Everyone in my life sends me incredibly long emails – my mom, and you, for two examples."

"Yes, my recent ones have been really long."

"And interesting and great to read," he eagerly asserts. "I compose responses in my head as I read along, but by the time I reach the end I've lost the energy to reply."

My heart sinks. I send up a small life raft of hope. "I know if I ever really need to hear back from you, I can ask and you'll respond, right?"

"Yes, absolutely," he confirms.

# BECAUSE I'M ME...

I have drafted, edited, and rewritten an email to Mr. Lucky and given it five different subject headings so far. But I haven't hit send. I will before I go to bed.

Because I'm me.

Even though I have wise counsel advising me to wait—until morning, until he returns from his trip, until he seeks me out again if I am shrouded in silence—I'm not waiting. None of which is wrong, it's just not me.

I'm proud that I waited this long to email him. Yes I realize it's less than 24 hours. I talked to several people about all of this today. Partly, I felt silly for seeking so much support, but I'm hurt and confused about our conversation last night.

My body is sore today. These delightful aches remind me of our evening together. But my heart hurts worse. His words stung. I don't believe in his indifference for a second.


Thu, Dec 12, 2013 at 10:54 PM
Last night was deliciously fun. Thank you for crafting another creative, sexy, interesting scene.

Will you please clarify what you meant when you said, "We've had a good run..." because it came off as indifferent and dismissive, neither of which resonate with me based on any other aspect of our connection.

I understand and accept that you don't know when or even if we will play again. I genuinely respect that and expected it (more when we will play again than if.)

What I did not expect was to feel dismissed by you. My best guess is that you felt defensive or nervous, which led you to make that statement.

What we've shared together, so far, doesn't warrant indifference.

Please do respond to this before you travel.

> *Fri, Dec 13, 2013 at 7:22 AM*
> *I'm not entirely sure what you imply with dismissive.*
>
> *What I meant was: if we don't have another play scene, it's good that we managed to fit in six sessions, which gave us scope to explore a lot of interesting activities and situations.*

Fri, Dec 13, 2013 at 10:42 AM
Thank you for responding so quickly.

When you said, "we've had a good run..." it stung; I wanted reassurance.

I liken it to how hard it was for me to obey the command to not look at you while scening that night. Even as you praised me while sucking your cock, telling me in words that I was pleasing you, I wanted reassurance in a different way - I wanted to see it in your eyes. Not being allowed to was challenging in a way that worked well for me in scene. (And I recognize that my wanting to see that in your eyes does not mean it would be there were I permitted to look.)

I believe that what we have done together matters to you; you have shown me that repeatedly through your actions, attention, and engagement particularly in scene, which is why the statement you made felt dissonant.

I haven't landed on better words for how I experienced it than dismissive and indifferent. It seemed of no consequence to you whether we play together again. What I wanted, if it was true, was to know that even though there is uncertainty about our play in the future, that you value it and want it to continue. You might not feel that or might be unwilling to say it. I'm not asking you to answer that here.

I wish I'd been able to respond to your comment at the time, but my reaction was visceral, and I lost my words. All I could manage was to assert, later in the conversation, what is already obvious: I don't want that to be the last time we play. It is good that we have played together six times and explored interesting activities and situations. I concur. I was craving effusiveness and what I got was matter of fact.

Does that help you understand what I meant? Do you have thoughts about or reactions to what I've shared here?

Again, I would appreciate a response as soon as you are able.

*Fri, Dec 13, 2013 at 5:56 PM*
*I think I understand what you are saying and I'm sorry that I made you feel dismissed and hurt. A 'good run' was meant as a celebration of our success in finding a way to meet some of our complementary needs. A lot of people*

*don't get that chance.*

*Unfortunately, I'm a pretty cold fish; effusiveness is not on the menu. I enjoy our play, our connection, and our conversations both electronic and in person. I hope to continue to do so. But in a way, it's important to me that I make sure that it is of little consequence if we play again or not.*

*I don't know what changes are coming in my life, but I sense them, and I don't let the past or the future break my heart.*

*I hope that we have a chance to play again, whether the toys be word game tiles or handcuffs.*

Fri, Dec 13, 2013 at 8:20 PM
Thank you for your responsiveness. Your apology soothed me.

I understand better what you meant by a 'good run' now.

A cold fish, eh? Not entirely. And yes, I know, effusiveness is not on the menu - sadly that doesn't inherently curb my desire for it. Thankfully, plenty of what is on the menu pleases my palate. Hearing explicitly how you feel about our play, our connection, and our conversations allays my doubt.

The guardedness you describe in making sure that it is of little consequence whether we play again resonates with what I felt the other night. I understand it now, in light of your uncertainty about upcoming changes.

I wish I understood more about what variables affect our chances to play again - in any sense of the word, but that isn't a discussion for now. And I imagine I'm not the only one who desires that clarity.

Here's wishing you a fantastic trip overseas. May you get lots of writing done on the plane. I hope you enjoy your time reconnecting with your partner. Travel safely.

Thank you again for your attentiveness to this exchange, especially right before leaving.

# CRASHING

This crisis wind has blown through, leaving strands of sadness and anger in its wake. I am calmer today. Now that I understand that he isn't indifferent, I mourn the loss of the rest of that evening curled beside him. It might not have been my last chance, but if it was, I'm heartbroken that our misunderstanding stole my words and my chance to be close to him. My body pulled away to protect me. I wish when my voice recovered that night, my bravery would have reset itself too. Of course, he could have asked; he clearly noticed my disengagement.

But anger at him doesn't soothe me. I'd rather pine for him, torture myself with sweet memories, and hold onto a wisp of hope that this isn't how our ending is written. When his words came crashing down around me last week, I went numb. I crawled inside myself. Backing away from him, I gave myself permission to feel jilted, hurt, stunned. Then, I boxed up my emotions and tucked them away as we sat together on the love seat – him facing ahead, me turned sideways toward him, pointedly not touching.

"Did you paint all these?" I inquired, calmer than I felt. Two or three things in the room became sentence starters for me as I fumbled for vocal footing. I wish I'd said what the fuck did you mean by that and why did you say it? I wanted to bare my hurt and anger in the moment. But I didn't.

We chatted. I told stories and listened to his. I offered warm feedback on the beautiful night we'd shared. Then we said goodbye.

He walked me to my car and we hugged again; I was too buttoned up to feel anything like the desperation I'd expect if that was indeed our last embrace.

I drove home, tired, cold from the inside out, as the hurt dislodged itself from the corner of my heart where I'd exiled it.

The next day I told my incredulous story of the conversation gone wrong to everyone who would listen - what he said, how I lost my voice. More than once I started with a request for my listener not to hate him, because I'd feel compelled to defend him and I was too hurt to go there. Time and again I was met with empathy and understanding that soothed my broken heart. But my friends were angry that he would treat me this way.

I consulted my mentors and support people: Gayle, Summer, and Calvin. I needed outside input before I challenged him in writing. And the calendar loomed. By Thursday, there were only two days before he left the country for over a week. I didn't want to be rash, but I knew my window for getting a response was closing.

Picking myself up from this crisis meant reaching out for support, being heard and validated. And then it meant emailing him.

There is still uncertainty, but less fear.

# GRAVITY

It's been a week. A week ago right now I was at his house making conversation with him on the love seat, actively avoiding the reality that I might never submit to him again, might never again feel him inside me, might never feel his lips on mine. Ever.

Today, I finished with my last client, did some paperwork, then looked at the clock and realized it was 8:01 pm. My body trembled as I remembered that exactly a week ago, I had just entered his house to begin our scene.

Thankfully, tonight, I had a good distraction in hanging out with Calvin. We went out to consult about client work but ended up talking about personal stuff for each of us. I see Gayle tomorrow and also have women's group; I know I can talk about this in both of those places, but I have no idea what to say.

There are the facts: I got hurt; it might be over; I feel angry at him; I don't want it to be over, I don't know what is happening; I feel sad. I have theories about what's going on for him, what he might be feeling, why he might want to be done with our connection.

There were moments today when the thought that we might never play together again rolled through me without unhinging my heart. Whatever I felt, it wasn't paralyzing or catastrophic. I'm angry at him for not initiating the conversation about our future before we played that night. He knew for weeks that I felt uncertain about how his partner coming home would affect us. Instead of engaging with me about that, he'd said it was too much for him to process. Did he mean to imply that he'd process it later? We talked about a couple of minor things after our scene last week, but only because I brought them up.

I've been thinking about what sort of contact I want with him when he returns. Of course I want to play again. But before that, we need to talk. There's a list of questions in my head: How will he keep me in the loop about our future? Will he talk with me in person about what's going on? I don't want to do that processing via email, I need to be able to see his eyes, hear his inflection. Email won't suffice.

# MELANCHOLY

How do I separate out the general loneliness I feel from my longing for him? The ocean of my desire is bigger than he is willing to hold.

Only one time in the last year have I gone to sleep in the arms of a lover. Most nights I'm alone in bed, holding my pillow or stuffed lion for comfort, so that my arms aren't bereft of connection. Otherwise I snuggle my daughter as she falls asleep in the warm comfort of my embrace, precisely the way I wish to sleep in someone else's arms.

Shopping for dates online feels futile and hopeless. Yes, the connections I've made there so far have been interesting and somewhat fruitful. But will I ever find the love that I seek online? I found Mr. Lucky there, and a couple other dates, none of whom panned out to be available for what I want, or wanted me in the way I desire and deserve.

I miss Mr. Lucky. This distance is grueling and there is no end in sight.

Today, at a Christmas event, I will spend time with extended family, make small talk, answer the same questions over and over as I visit with each new person. As I prepare the sound bites I'll share, I ask myself how much truth I'm willing to tell. *Busy, happy, doing well* those are what people want to hear. *Lonely, seeking love, melancholy...* people aren't prepared to absorb those answers. Yet they're just as true as the other descriptions of my life. What will I say? How much truth can I let pass in service of being authentic? How visible will I allow myself to be? Is it really the wrong time to take up drinking at family events?

# IMPATIENT

This is the voice of impatience, the subtext of any email I might send him from this anxious state of mind: Hey! Hey! Remember me? I miss you. Do you miss me? Of course you don't. But I miss you! How was Europe? How's your partner? Have you talked with her about me yet? Hey, I miss you! Did I mention that? Did you get any writing done on the plane? Ooh ooh, those things we did last time we played were so fun, especially this and this and this. How is it to be home and have your partner living there with you? What are you doing for Christmas? Want to play dominoes soon? I went out to karaoke with friends tonight. Want to go to karaoke for my birthday with me and some friends? No, not 'til April. Please, still be in my life in April. I want you to karaoke at my party. And birthday spankings, I want those too. From you.

I'm still trying to wait until he contacts me first. So far I've made it to my goal of not emailing him before Christmas.

*Wed, Dec 25, 2013 at 6:19 AM*
*i hope the holidays are treating you well and you're having*
*good celebrations with the family, and low stress in*
*general, which can be hard this time of year.*

*things are interesting and positive around here - i'm back
from my trip and the household reintegration project is in
full swing. it surely is a lot of work, though ... trying to
build new healthy systems and get into good
communication patterns. my expectation is that, for now at
least, email is the only social feeler i have the availability
and energy for. i mention this to give you a realistic
expectation of the state of our connection from my side.*

*when things settle down, we should play some dominoes,
though.*

# GRASPING

I woke up on Christmas morning to an email from Mr. Lucky, written from his phone at 6:15 a.m. Jetlag much?!

His email felt warm and engaging but not effusive since that isn't on the menu. I appreciated his casual tone. It was a useful update on what is happening for him and his availability. And holy cow do I appreciate having a realistic expectation from his side of things.

The first thing I noticed as I lay in bed reading his email was my breathing; I felt more calm than I had since last hearing from him. I opened a blank email on my phone and typed *Yes, I will gratefully grasp at whatever kindness you visit upon me. The why of that is not hard to uncover.* Hours later, after my daughter had opened her presents and I was in the shower getting ready for Christmas breakfast, I realized I'm not losing him. He mentioned playing dominoes, which means we at least get to have that sort of interaction. Of course, the jury is still out on whether we get to scene again.

When I told Calvin about it at Christmas breakfast, he looked unimpressed and asked, "Was he being an asshole? Was the email two sentences long?" No need to wonder how Calvin feels about Mr. Lucky.

Calvin asked if I wrote back immediately. I told him I won't reply for at least one whole day. He lobbied for me to wait three days. That isn't happening.

Thu, Dec 26, 2013 at 10:40 PM
Welcome home! Thanks for emailing yesterday, it was good to hear from you.

Holiday family time has been mostly lovely with relatively little stress. Today I went to the casino with several siblings, cousins, and my parents. It was fun and I even won a little at the blackjack table! Hopefully your holiday time has been enjoyable too.

It's wonderful to hear that things are positive there. Yay! And yes, no shortage of work, all that reintegration and establishing systems and communication patterns. Valuable, rewarding, even enjoyable endeavors, but work nonetheless. Wishing you both well as you settle in.

Thank you for the clear expectation of how things look from your side. I look forward to dominoes when things settle down for you.

Two contrasting memories from our most recent scene have remained present to me. One was your disciplinary tone - exhibited many times that night, much to my delight. The other was the exquisite tenderness of drying you off after the shower. What a perfect vehicle for demonstrating my submissive devotion to you. I could have joyfully spent more time on that task, but rushed because of an imagined time constraint. Post-scene regrets are generally few for me, but I do wish I hadn't hurried through that moment. (Check it out! Just one paragraph of reflections [that I'm sharing here], instead of many pages. Maybe there's hope for me and brevity after all.)

# GRIEF COOKIES

To honor the fifteen year anniversary of my best friend Heather's death I've sequestered myself in a hotel room at the Oregon coast to write and read and cry. My room has a stunning view of Haystack Rock directly outside my patio. With the sliding door cracked open, I hear the hum and crash of the waves.

Tracey baked me cookies for my trip, something so uncharacteristically domestic of her. She handed them to me in a green and pink striped canister with a yellow knob at the top. "They're just the kind from store-bought dough that's scored into bite-sized chunks," she confessed. "But I know you'll be sad, and who doesn't want chocolate chip cookies for eating their feelings?"

I blinked back tears. Tracey and I shared overlapping stuff about food and weight. She understood – sister to sister, fat girl to fat girl. And she, more than anyone in my life, was there for me when Heather died.

Tucked into my hotel room, I immerse myself in words. The table becomes an altar. Candles flicker beside a vase full of bright pink heather blossoms, the same color as the sky when the sun sets at the other end of the ocean. In my old journal from when Heather died, I discover a passage that wasn't part of my conscious memory of that time period.

*I want to be by the ocean, to let the vast expanse of rolling blue wash over me and fill me with its rhythms, to teach me to trust in the wax and wane, to sing with me the songs that are her and us and me.*

Sometimes the story of Heather's death feels like the singular narrative of my life. Our decade of friendship spanned from age fourteen to twenty-four. I write that story again and again because it broke me apart and I am still, always, working to fit myself back together around the absence of her in my days. In my piece for Trifecta last week, I wrote:

*She is the perpetual referent of my grief. This myopic reverence belies myriad losses, nestled in my marrow, overflowing this basin of mourning. Mirrors, lost to distance or death, dazzle still though absent.*

It's almost mathematical. Grief is synonymous with Heather; they're one and the same in my vocabulary. Throughout the weekend, I snack on the cookies from Tracey, spilling crumbs across the pages of my journal. I eat every last cookie she sent. They taste like love.

# MISPLACED MISSING – AN EMAIL I'M NOT SENDING HIM

It's been a week since I wrote you back. My email was light and friendly to match your tone. I only asked one question, not out of deference to your limit but because I didn't want you to feel beholden.

I miss you. This week with New Year's and the anniversary of Heather's death, I long for physically intimate connection. I'm staying in a beautiful room on the coast with a view of the ocean and Haystack Rock. You and I could have all sorts of fun in the jacuzzi tub, glass-walled shower, and king size bed. I wish we could share this space – read, write, enjoy each other's company (and not just in sexy ways). But I know that kind of interaction isn't on the menu.

When we spoke about Heather's death, I told you the circumstances of it, but I don't remember if I told you when it happened. I don't expect you to know, but I wish you did. I wish it occurred to you to reach out to me during this week, but you don't have enough knowledge about the situation to know to do that. My hope is unfounded and my expectation unfair. Maybe you'll respond today or tomorrow anyway.

Once, when I told you I considered asking to play for the emotional catharsis of it, you said we could have, if I had inquired. You said you'd have done whatever you could to help. That offer doesn't stand under current circumstances. I wish it did. Touch and physical intensity would feel especially comforting right now.

You are on my mind, but it's less urgent; the longing isn't running away with me. Today, while throwing stones into the ocean for loved ones, I threw one in for you. It held a hybrid of intentions: for your overall well-being; for you and your partner as you settle into this cohabitation; and that we remain in each other's lives as friends, but also that we get to continue to play.

I'm holding you to your word about email contact. Although there weren't many direct questions in my last note to you, there was plenty to respond to, even briefly.

Mostly I hope to hear from you soon. I know that missing you isn't entirely about you. I also miss physical intimacy and sexual connection, and the intense energy between us.

# CONSEQUENCES

Seriously? If email is all he's available for, then fucking show up there! How hard is that? I'm not asking for a novella; I didn't even smother him with questions in my last email. So why the hell hasn't he written back?

I'm the one who wants what isn't available to me. Me. I'm doing that. I am trying to sit with that awareness without feeling shame about it. Yes, I am making this choice. No, it doesn't serve me all that well. And yes, I might stay here. I get to make that choice and live with the consequences of it. Today, one of those consequences is anger. There's nothing to do about this anger except acknowledge it and let it pass through me.

# ONE WAY TICKET TO WHATEVER

My protective friends are angling for me to move on, to say whatever already and walk away from this connection that is clearly bound for heartbreak. But I've no plans to book a ticket to whatever. My reader board lists departures for familiar routes: infatuation, unrequited love, dizzying desire, and, yes, heartbreak. They're each only a short hop on one of those puddle-jumper planes where every slight breeze jostles your sense of direction and balance, precisely the way my body reacts to his touch and the tenor of his voice.

I've probably earned enough miles from wayward crushes and ill-fated first dates to pay for a first-class ticket to Whatever. I could gather all the self-esteem, worthiness, and confidence that fit into my carry-on and jet off at a moment's notice. If I were willing.

Yet how could I possibly make that journey when his words call forth my own in ways that delight us both, igniting passion and devotion? When his hands on my body spark sizzling intensity? When his smile lights up my heart for days? When more of me is vibrantly alive in this relationship than I've been in over a decade?

If I were going to walk away, it would have happened when he seemed to casually profess indifference about our connection. In that moment, I disentangled myself from his embrace and moved to the opposite end of the couch, speechless and stunned. Even then, I refused to align myself with his dismissal. I challenged the dissonance between his words and his actions. It took two attempts before his defenses softened and he let me in, confirming what my heart and body already knew…what we do together matters to him, and so do I.

My friends still hope I'll pass through whatever before boarding a connecting flight to unexplored relationship frontiers. But for now, I'll continue to weather this particular turbulence. Even with a broken heart on the horizon, the in-flight entertainment is the best I've ever known.

# BANKING ON TOM

Yesterday I heard the tune to *You Don't Bring Me Flowers* in my head, with my own made up lyrics: *you don't play Tom Petty anymore…*

I have this thing about musical visitations. I even wrote about it for Trifecta one week:

*As the God of musical visitation, I minister to hearts torn asunder through all manner of loss. Attuned to their sorrows I deliver the song which offers grace and hope amidst unfathomable grief.*

Ever since Mr. Lucky and I met, I've associated him with Tom Petty. When I listen to the radio, I hear Petty's music regularly. It could just be that my favorite station (aptly named KINK) has a soft spot for him, but I prefer to take it as a sign from the universe that whatever this is with Mr. Lucky is still viable. Tom Petty is currently avoiding me on the airwaves.

Today, I caught the end of a set, as the DJ announced the artists up next. I was distracted and listened to the ads during the music break. When the next song started, sure enough, it was Tom Petty. I smiled, said out loud to myself and to the universe, *Yeah? Well then show me. Write me back. Stay engaged.*

It's been two weeks since I've heard from Mr. Lucky. I'm antsy, but not angsty, an important distinction in my world. I want to know how he is and when we can see each other. But my world doesn't hinge on it. I believe I'll hear from him, at some point. I just have zero control over it. So I'll take the visitation from Tom with a smile on my face and go about my day.

# STEPPING AWAY SLIGHTLY

From our first interaction, I've been cloaked in a shroud of desire and devotion to Mr. Lucky. Often, wearing this metaphorical garment is intoxicating. Today it feels heavy, bulky, and excessive.

I give myself permission to embody and claim my desire to be in this connection with him, even against the concerned caution of those who love me. I said to Summer earlier today that I need to allow myself to be present in this, against all odds, in order to unwind from it.

I am by no means done with him. But I'm ready to back down from this plateau of intensity where I've been idling.

Fri, Jan 10, 2014 at 4:49 PM
How are things? You're on my mind today so I decided to say hello.

My new year is off to a positive start. I went to the coast for a mini-retreat and it was a great gift of time to myself for reading, writing, and honoring the 15 year anniversary of Heather's death.

My writing year started on the right foot by placing third in the first writing challenge of the year. The best part was sharing the winner's circle with two of my favorite writers from the Trifecta community.

That's the news from my corner of Portland. I hope things continue to be interesting and positive for you.

*Sun, Jan 12, 2014 at 12:21 PM*
*I'd been drafting a short email to you to find out what the news was over your way. Thanks for pre-empting.*

*Your mini-retreat sounds awesome and thoughtful, and like a great way to kick off a good year.*

*There's lots of busyness going on here, including unfortunately a breakdown on the non-monogamy machine. It's temporarily disabled while we work on repairs. Sharing a house and integrating lives is more continual hard work than I expected.*

*I'm glad you're having fun adventures and doing good work!*

# I AM A PERSON WHO...

I am a person who connects, who collects people like stones at the ocean. Once the tendrils of my love and interest take hold, I'm reluctant to let go. When I reach into the soul of another and am met there I bathe in the communion.

I am also a person who turns each moment, every ounce of conversation over again and again in my mind. Sometimes more of the relationship happens within my own brain than in actual interactions with the other person. He becomes my own creation, and that disparity creates disappointing dissonance. Of course he lets me down, because the man I created in my mind is not real. I magnify the parts of him I adore and downplay what doesn't suit me.

Really, at the root of it, he's just a man – not a god or a hero, not even the most fascinating man I know. He is human and he is letting go. I can choose to let go too and see what is next, or I can hold tight to the Mr. Lucky in my head and linger there, alone.

It isn't remotely clear to me how to finish being in love with him. I know it's time to gather the tangled remains of my feelings for him and move on. But how? I was never supposed to drown in my affection for him.

Clear the fog. Feel your pulse. Breathe. In. Out. Again and again. Follow the beat of your heart. Let yourself sink to the depths and float on the crest of these waves. You gave yourself permission to relish every other aspect of this. Do the same now. Breathe in the sting of regret. Listen to the wail of anguish. Taste the delicious remnants of intensity. And then end the scene, find a way to close it, for now if not forever.

Thu, Jan 16, 2014 at 11:19 PM
More continual hard work than you expected sounds rough. And it's never fun when machines we enjoy malfunction.

Could we please get together to talk over a game of dominoes or a word game? It would help me to have some context and a better understanding of what to expect in our connection. Plus it would be nice to see you. I'm traveling in early February and getting together before then would be best for me, if that is possible.

Aside from busyness and working hard in your relationship, how are you?

# BLAST OFF

Why am I still waiting for him to count us down to the formidable end? One, two, three, four, five, six days of silence from him. I generally defer to his timing, wait patiently or not, but bide my time either way. Today I woke up angry, frustrated, and hurt. For the first time I considered being the one to blast off on my own, launch myself out of this tedious, tense anticipation.

I want to lash out, turn the tables, scold him for being rude and disrespectful. Damn! Is it any wonder those are the words I spat at my daughter this morning? I have no available venue for wielding this anger at him – he isn't willing to engage. Is his silence supposed to be my answer? No, we can't get together to talk, there is nothing to discuss. But his silence could mean other things, ranging from procrastination to negotiation. I can't know until (unless) he reaches back.


Fri, Jan 24, 2014 at 4:55 PM
I accept that responding to email can be challenging for you. I wonder about the state of things for you because you and your experience matter to me.

What am I to infer from your lack of response? This silence feels painful and confusing.

Several months ago you said something to the effect of, "Right, I can just talk to Meg, she understands." That remains true. Without knowing the details, I have empathy and compassion for the challenges of combining households and the ongoing negotiations involved. And I continue to wish both of you well through that process.

I asked a direct question, I'd appreciate a direct answer - even if there is no simple answer. So again, can we please get together to talk? Please do respond to this email.

# THE ONE I WANTED TO SEND
# BUT DIDN'T

Mr. Lucky-
You're being an ass by not responding to me. Please don't punk
out on me this way, it doesn't suit you and I deserve more respect
than this.
Meg

# PREOCCUPIED AND ANXIOUS

What the hell is going on with Mr. Lucky and why he hasn't written me back yet? I've asked that question a zillion times, but this feels different. Especially after repeating my request for a response. I want to still believe in his integrity and in the sanctity of what we shared. I want to think he respects me.

What will I do if he doesn't write me? Will I text or call him? Would that make me a stalker. I'll admit to a little online stalking of him. There was a handful of places to find him online, but he took down his dating profile and hasn't done anything on BDSM sites for a long time. So only his regular social media page is left.

This is what I want:
I want him to write me back before the weekend is over.
I want him to apologize for his silence.
I want to know what's going on.
I want to meet and talk.
I want to know that he is advocating for the space to interact with me.
I want to be his friend.
I want to continue writing with him.
I want to play with him again.

# SOME OF THE THINGS I WANT TO SAY AND PROBABLY WON'T

I know you don't like to be told what to do, and that my asking more than once for you to respond might feel like that. I still deserve the bare minimum respect of a reply. If you intend this to be the end, say that directly instead of expecting me to infer it from your silence. If you know me at all, you comprehend how excruciating this is for me. Radio silence feels like cruel torture.

You were so fucking clear on Christmas about setting realistic expectations. If that's what you were trying to do with the broken non-monogamy machine bit, it didn't fucking work. If what you really meant is that you aren't going to be in contact with me at all, I deserve to have that spelled out.

And what sucks is I believe you know that. You had a play partner break up with you by email not long ago, and you told me it hurt your feelings. Because of that, I assumed you wouldn't do that to me. And this is worse – you aren't even communicating; you've just checked out. Part of the hurt is the idea that it's over between us, but not having definitive communication is so much more painful for me.

# TRIFECTA – WEEK #101

Immersed in distraction, I wordlessly swallow this acrid grief.

Intimate intersections, once delicately tangled,

have disintegrated within your excruciating silence.

# HOW TO NOT BE A TOTAL PUNK IN A RELATIONSHIP

Consistency is a great place to start. If in one message you make a point to set clear expectations about your availability, don't then hide behind a clever, vacuous metaphor in your next communication.

Freezing the other party out with unexpected radio silence is cruel and unusual punishment. Have the decency and basic respect to tell someone if you plan to stop communicating.

Know your audience. Recognize that silence will be exquisitely hurtful to an overly analytical, word-focused therapist who communicates for a living. Since you claim to not be that sort of sadist, check your intentions.

Keep your agreements. When you've verbally consented to provide prompt responses when asked directly, follow through. Otherwise every shred of integrity once ascribed to you might perish.

# STARLIGHT

You were privy to the me that is starlight as I rearranged myself into constellations of connection, attraction, attention, desire. I offered you tender, spiraled intensity as I stood whole in myself and trusted that I was enough. You saw the lion in me, recognized my strength of body and character. You met me there, my wild hunger tempered by your cool, creative command. Our words and bodies merged, melody and harmony, until this dissonant silence. Radiant orange passion melted into cold blue absence.

Now I scramble to regain my footing and remember the textures of my own luminous self. I will myself to believe again that I am whole, strong, sweet, and beloved.

This is the pitiful stage of grief where commonplace objects have the power to quiver my lip and wet my eyes with sentimental sorrow. My heart lurches at every ordinary reminder of this lost love. I am seemingly surrounded by things reminiscent of him – art, bicycles, words, books.

I ache to be done, to propel myself gently through this grieving so I can reach the distant shore of solace.

# WHAT TO DO IF YOU'VE ALREADY ACTED LIKE A PUNK

Apologize, but only if you know how and only if you mean it. For the record: I'm sorry that you _____ is not an apology, no matter what fills in that blank. Here are some examples just because they're fun to write. *I'm sorry that you overreacted. I'm sorry that you misunderstood me. I'm sorry that you felt angry.*

A true apology means taking responsibility for your actions, and a true apology often begins with either I'm sorry that I _____, or I'm sorry for _____. *I'm sorry that I lost my temper. I'm sorry for yelling at you when I was actually upset at my boss. I'm sorry for not e-mailing you back sooner.*

Empathize before (or instead of) explaining. Understand that empathy doesn't mean you agree with the other person, only that you care about how they feel. *Wow, if I thought I wouldn't hear back from you again, I would feel sad and angry too.* Pay attention to what specific needs are being presented to you. Do your best to stay on topic and respond directly to those requests.

Make clear agreements that you are willing and able to keep, or don't make any at all. Especially if previous punk behavior included breaking an agreement, this part is essential. Unless integrity is of no consequence to you.

Fri, Jan 31, 2014 at 12:21 AM
When I get no response to my emails, I feel hurt and sad, because I have strong needs for communication and respect (for me as a person and for the connection we've shared.)

It seems you would recognize how your silence would be excruciating for me. Please don't do this anymore. Please respond, even if you don't know what to say, or you don't have any definitive answers. I'm more interested in a conversation and some context than in answers. And I don't deserve to be ignored.

You were so clear in your email on Christmas about setting realistic expectations. Where was that commitment to clarity in your clever metaphor about the non-monogamy machine being broken and temporarily closed for repair? If what you really meant by that is that you are not able or willing to be in contact with me, I deserve to have you spell that out. One could argue that your silence should be interpreted as the answer to my question about your willingness to engage. I am reluctant to accept that answer.

Your email on Christmas led me to believe that we could continue as friends. The broken machine metaphor offered me maddeningly little clarity on what is possible. And your lack of response since then remains confusing, hurtful, and disappointing, especially given the verbal agreement you made to respond to me if I specifically asked you to do so.

Although my investment in this connection carried more intensity than yours all along, I trust that you care about me and it is not your intention to hurt me. Your integrity and attunement are two things I have been grateful for since we met. I have worked hard to process my feelings and my distress about this lack of communication elsewhere, out of a desire not to visit my emotional process on you.

Will you please engage in a conversation with me in some form (in person, phone, email) where you show up and share with me some context and information?

Once again, I leave to travel on February 4th. Receiving communication from you prior to that would be appreciated.

*Fri, Jan 31, 2014 at 5:43 PM*
*Ah, Meg, you're killing me! Every time you email I start frantically working on a reply, hoping to placate your need for communication, and reassure you that things-are-okay-here-but-it's-just-a-bad-time, then trail off in a fog of inadequacy. Then I pick it up the next day and go through the cycle again.*

*To have you perceive that as disrespect is sad and understandable. Sorry, pal! I'm not at all interested in causing you pain of that sort.*

*Anyway, I'm struggling with a lot right now. Every day is a metaphorical death march of cold air, endless work, lifestyle adjustments, and early bedtimes. I cannot sustain the effort involved in managing our connection up to the level (that I think) you want, although I find said connection pleasant and valuable.*

*Thanks as always for your empathy, compassion, and friendship, which come through clearly in all your communications. I appreciate them and only hope you receive back some echo in my own sparse replies.*

Sun, Feb 2, 2014 at 12:20 AM
{Written in a tone of genuine amusement.} Dude, seriously?! You
make me wait two weeks for a response of any sort,
and I'm killing you?! That's funny!

Thank you for writing me back.

While I detest the sound of you cycling through a fog of
inadequacy, it's comforting to know that responding to me is on
your mind. What keeps you from sending the replies? What are
you afraid of? (Especially when reassurance is exactly what I seek.)
It may or may not surprise you that I have an overactive
imagination with a weakness for hyperbole, which spent much of
the last two weeks feeding me thoughts like: He wants absolutely
nothing to do with me. I'm never ever going to hear from him
again. He is as good as dead to me. Fun times. The only good
thing has been the writing I've produced from it. You should
know that I am wildly grateful for all the ways in which our
connection has fueled my writing.

I'd strongly prefer something imperfect, brief, and timely than to
wait and wait without hearing from you at all. Both because I
hate waiting and also because now that I know about your frantic
reply drafting and inadequacy cycling, I don't want you
experiencing that. This reminds me of the first email you sent me,
with the question about what sort of scenes interest me. I
answered that question for you quickly, in a clear, comprehensive
way, revealing intimate information about myself...all with
absolutely zero trust established between us. I invite you to lean
into the trust, rapport and connection we've since built and to
take risks in responding to me. Nearly any response you send
would be easier to swallow than that dreadful extended silence.
And to be clear, if I'd known there would be a long interim
before you responded, I wouldn't have panicked.

I know that responding to email can overwhelm you which is
why I've been specific about what I'm asking of you. It is also

why I keep inquiring about talking in person or by phone. I might need to resort to another survey to actually get the answers I seek. (Sorry, NSA, this one isn't nearly as salacious as the first one!)

Here goes:
1) Can we talk sometime? _____ yes    _____ no
2) If answer to question #1 is yes, which works better for you? _____ in person    _____ phone
3) Any guess as to when this could happen? _____ no,  _____ I am not sure _____ no sooner than 2 weeks
4) Which factors are roadblocks to this happening (check all that apply):
_____ my level of interest in talking with you
_____ negotiating about contact with you
_____ scheduling logistics
_____ inability or unwillingness to commit to a plan
_____ general overwhelm in my life
_____ other:

_____

It's good to hear that you aren't interested in disrespecting me, thank you. Sigh, I do miss the kind of pain you enjoy causing me.

See, you write stuff like metaphorical death march of cold air, endless work, lifestyle adjustments, and early bedtimes and it piques my curiosity and empathy every time. I wish things weren't so rough for you right now. I hope there are pockets of creativity, adventure, passion, and joy intermingled with the daily slog of challenges.

I dispute the premise that the issue is the level of connection I want. I believe it's at least as much the pressure you feel to manage our connection in a certain way - and not all of that pressure comes from me.

You haven't met the level of connection I want in months.

What I want and what is available are divergent, that's nothing new. I continue to choose limited connection with you over not having you in my life at all. As long as I have any say in that equation I am likely to land there.

It's gratifying that my empathy, compassion, and friendship come through clearly. Thank you for stating this explicitly. I often experience echoes back in your replies.

My expectations for your responses are fairly low. I write long messages to you because I generally have a lot to say and my sense is that you have space to receive material, it's the responding that trips you up. (Please correct that assumption if I'm wrong.) I haven't expected in-depth replies from you for a long time now, regardless of how involved my communication to you is, and regardless of how much I miss having access to more of you. Again, that is why I see meeting up in person as a better option than relying on email. You admitted that it felt good (and out of character and exhausting) to talk that night I came over at the end of September. I can only imagine that to be more palatable than weeks of spiraling inadequacy as you try to reply to my email before I pre-empt you, again.

Before we played in December, I wanted to ask that if you ever knew it might be our last time playing that you let me know beforehand. But I didn't want to initiate that conversation because I never want it to be the last time. Having learned from that experience, I am asking specifically that if you reach a point where you are not able or willing to be in my life at all, will you please communicate that with me directly, in person? I remember you saying that a play partner had broken up with you abruptly via email and how it hurt your feelings.

It would devastate me if you walked away abruptly without my getting to say goodbye to you.

As I send off this email to you, I am feeling calm. I'm not stressed out about hearing back from you and I hope you can avoid feeling frantic about writing me back.

# TRUTH-TELLING

It's time to do a little truth-telling with myself. Calvin and I are on our way to a six-day clinical training on shame and vulnerability – this seems like an appropriate opportunity for some raw honesty.

What did I really feel when submitting to Mr. Lucky? Why did it thrill me to serve him, fold his clothes, make his bed? Because I got to be in his presence. I got to matter to him.

I hate the words he used in his email – placate, pleasant, valuable. Yeah, this is valuable to you, asshole, because I worship you. I comfort you. I hang on your every word and offer you focused attention and heartfelt empathy laced with love and devotion. What isn't valuable in that?

So what do I get from this? Writing. Love, lust, devotion, sex, heartbreak, grief and loss – this is where my writing fire burns brightest. He's been a catalyst to intense experience, depth of emotion, and to some of my strongest writing to date.

So, truth telling. What did I love about playing with him? I just forced myself to write that sentence in the past-tense. The chances of us playing again are so negligible it's irresponsible of me to harbor even a shred of hope about it. I rail against that with every ounce of my desire, but I have to proceed as if that is true.

He will never – *no, damn it, I don't want to write that.*

He might never, *there, I can tolerate that.*

He might never kiss me. I may never submit to him again, pour him wine, kiss his feet or lie before him. I already miss the weight of him across my back, holding me in place. I crave the sharp sting of his hand across my face.

I might never again be his.

And he was never, not even for an instant, mine.

# WARDROBE

It's a story I've told so many times, but here are the parts I tend to leave out.

As she sits there, huddled under the comforter on my bed, Tracey argues with me about the object of my current obsession. "Why would you settle for this guy who doesn't treat you with respect? Why not date someone who is kind to you, who has time and wants *you*?"

I try to counter, to explain again how amazing Mr. Lucky is, how when we're together he's present and attentive. "He's sexy and he *does* want me," I insist. I attempt to distract her with the task at hand – which shirt with which skirt for my conference? Do I really need five pairs of shoes for a week-long conference on shame and vulnerability?

Flustered, I turn the tables on her. "But what about you, Trace – what are you looking for in your dating life?"

Her response is subtle, only alarming well after the fact. "I don't know that I'm going to make it." I take in her unwashed hair that stands up at odd angles, the sweatshirt she's likely been wearing all week. Her face is expressionless. Her words are a loose thread that I notice, but leave untouched.

She throws a pair of leggings at me, hits me in the chest with them. "Put these on with that black tank top and the purple cardigan." Apparently next up is a lesson in leggings. "You think you need to wear a skirt over these to cover your butt, right?"

"Yeah, it's more comfortable that way," I admit.

"But you don't need to, your legs look great and they seem so much longer without a skirt cutting them in half."

I do what she says, and she's right, in that annoying know-it-all big sister way. I take notes as she packs my suitcase so I'll remember what to wear when I get to San Antonio for the conference. Without her help I'd have packed jeans and black t-shirts, maybe one skirt with a black and grey striped shirt, and definitely only one pair of shoes. No color, no variety. Dull, boring, safe.

Safety. I'm not attuned to Tracey's physical risk. I don't know her edge is so close.

Every day of the conference I post photos on social media to show that I'm following her instructions about my outfits. I even wear the ones most outside my comfort zone early in the week instead of hiding in my drab, casual clothes. I call her from the balcony of my hotel overlooking the San Antonio Riverwalk to gush about the conference.

"I've met amazing therapists from all over the country. The days are long but full of connection. And everything is more fun with Calvin. We're learning all about shame resilience and how to show up as our most authentic self." Tracey listens but she's quiet and subdued, distracted.

When we talk I'm careful with my language, make myself swallow my usual phrases about her day going well or whether she's having fun, because that isn't the tenor of her days. Her stories fall flat, there's not much to tell from inside her depression.

That thread from before snags at me, unravels all the way through my chest as the weight sinks in. I can feel the bottom edge of her words, can sense what she might mean. She's desperately unhappy and can't find her way out of it.

"Our break is over, Trace, it's time to go back in for our next session," I tell her. "I'll catch up with you tomorrow." She hangs up and I listen to the silence for one more second.

*Thu, Feb 6, 2014 at 9:16 AM*
*i'm hearing that any reply is almost as important as a good reply, so this email is entirely communication, but no information. it's intended to acknowledge receipt of your latest novella, and to say that i am working on a good reply.*

*your handmade survey form is endearingly crazy!*

*i hope you're doing some good learning and teaching down there.*

# CROCUS

Walking toward the elevator on a break from the training, I casually scroll through new emails. Mr. Lucky's name catches my eye. I've spent entire days willing a message from him to spontaneously appear in my inbox, to no avail. Today, when I least expect one, it arrives.

Stunned, I cautiously open the message, scan it quickly before abruptly moving on. The elevator arrives and I climb aboard. At the eighth floor the doors open and I hop out, ready for a snippet of solitude in my room before heading back for afternoon sessions of the training.

I open Mr. Lucky's message again, absorb each line thoroughly this time.

He heard me.

*Deep breath.*

He paid attention.

*Sigh of relief.*

He met my request.

*Another deep breath.*

He found my message endearing.

A sliver of joy blooms in me like the tentative bud of a February crocus. If he's capable of meeting me like this, why won't he do it more? If he knows how to hear me and respond in kind, why does he freeze me out in silence? I long to take shelter in the subtle embrace of his words, but instead I trample the hopeful crocus bud, determined to stave off the pain of only getting what I want from him in insufficient, infrequent doses.

# EXPLICATE

It was going to be fantastic. I let the prompt word marinate in the back of my mind, so it might permeate the swirling intensity of my life and facilitate a powerful piece of writing. I let myself ruminate on how we seem caught between my desire to resuscitate and your urge to vacate what remains of our relationship. Somehow, I hoped it would perfectly illuminate what I want to communicate about the ways in which this relationship asks me to excavate my soul. Maybe, if written right, it could motivate you to fully participate instead of attempting to placate my needs, even if that would complicate your current situation.

One sentence inspired me to kick this prompt poetry slam style, rhyming each line around the word explicate. It would have been great. I brainstormed a list of thirty-three rhyming words and set to work. But I'm not a spoken word poet. I love that all of those words rhyme and think it would be fantastic to craft them into a piece that rocks a solid meter and could navigate these emotions.

So I'll let the sentence that started it all stand on its own: *Our connection is a poem that I want you to explicate.*

Sun, Feb 9, 2014 at 11:33 PM
Thank you for your email. I feel heard and respected and look forward to the good reply.

If my survey form is in the neighborhood of crazy, I'll definitely take the endorsement of endearing.

I arrived back to the ice and snow madness that is Portland late tonight. My trip was incredible and exhausting. Your comment about me teaching as well as learning made me smile.

I hope you are well.

# CALM OR TEMPEST?

This is a moment of calm before either another tempest or the end of it all. Anxiety has been woven into this connection from its inception. I've spent more time waiting for contact from him than I have in his presence.

Time twists and bends back upon itself in waves of paradox. When we're together, time is oceanic; I am buoyant in the sultry intensity of his touch, the tenor of his voice, the interplay of words and desire, power and surrender. When it's my turn to respond in our ongoing back and forth tether, there is a lull for me in this endless unbearable longing.

He has promised more words to come – without a due date, of course. I tread water, fearing the eventual heartbreak that is the only possible end to this affair.

# CLAMORING

Beneath the cloak of this longing is a shivering layer of sorrow.

Clamoring for shelter from his silence,

mourning the focused ferocity of his touch,

I am adrift on an ocean of grief.

*Fri, Feb 14, 2014 at 9:17 PM*
*(this is still in the spirit of sending something your way*
*whether it's polished or not.)*

*welcome back! i am still pondering your survey form.*

*i will certainly let you know if i think there's no chance of*
*us having a future connection. since i've not done so, you*
*can take it as clear that i wish to maintain our connection*
*and have hopes of finding a way to do so that is acceptable*
*to both of us.*

Mon, Feb 17, 2014 at 9:41 AM
Thanks for the email. I appreciate you responding even when things don't feel polished.

The survey's purpose was to inhibit pondering in favor of decisive answers. And to make you laugh. I'm sure you'll respond to it when you are ready.

I'm grateful for the clarity about your desire to continue our connection. I look forward to figuring out together what works.

How are you? Any of the death march intensity easing up?

# VIRTUAL

In this vacuous virtual connection there is no room for the real things I hoped would happen. No room to invite you to my karaoke birthday party or to my reading the day after my birthday. No birthday spankings that you'd deliver thoughtfully and make me count at least twice. Virtual doesn't hold any of that. Virtual doesn't hold anything right now because you don't exist there. You're not present. I don't know what the fuck you're doing, but you're not showing up.

Fri, Mar 7, 2014 at 11:06 AM
I could really use an update. Is there still a good reply in the works? How about answers to my survey?

I miss you. I'd like to know how you are. I'd like some contact with you. What would you like?

*Fri, Mar 7, 2014 at 7:25 PM*
*how time flies, meg!*

*here's the unfinished email i hoped to get sent before you prompted it.*

*I'm okay, thanks, but definitely in a transitional place. The death march is improving, but there's still plenty of general malaise and stressors around.*

*after another long delay I'm getting some slight clarity in my thoughts. you asked what i'd like: right now i'd like everyone to leave me alone and stop asking me for things (effort, time, opinions, changes, work, etc) while i figure out how i want my life organized and how much i choose to give.*

*i read a dan savage column recently that reinforced my feeling that i am not being fair in my communications with you. so i'll spare you the part about how i feel bad about this and so forth.*

*given the place i'm currently in, i'm trying to find realistic ideas about possibilities, thus:*

*here's what i can do:*
*desultory email, to keep in touch as friends. i think you're cool and interesting.*
*appreciate and/or constructively criticize any writing samples you choose to share*

*here's what i can't do:*
*meet, in the foreseeable future*
*function as a reliable communicant*

*as always, i hope you are well.*

*just fyi, i was making a mental list the other day of the ways we played that i thought went best — top three: the shower scene, the long wait tied on the bed, the second lunchtime session in general.*

Mon, Mar 10, 2014 at 12:53 AM
Happy to hear that the death march is improving. There's so much I want to know about this transitional place, but you've not made it accessible to me, nor do I expect you will. Hope and expectation are different animals.

Damn, I know that feeling of wanting everyone to leave me alone. You sound pretty stressed out, which makes my heart ache a little. Also, I recognize I'm culpable in contributing to this experience.

Thank you for the clarity of what you can do. I don't like any of the definitions of desultory I found, except maybe casual. (Another new word for me!)

(This was my initial reaction to the list of what you can't do.)

> *Can't, won't, isn't willing, doesn't want to, isn't allowed to, can't be bothered. I want to crawl inside this answer and tear it apart until I understand what he means. I wanted to know whether, but I also crave why. It wouldn't change the end result but I want it broken down into its individual components. I want percentages, fractions, atomic building blocks of his reasoning. I am petulant. I want to argue, push, and fight against his answer.*

I don't like thinking I might not see you again, and I don't comprehend how you measure the foreseeable future. I miss you. Of course, I miss the play too. I hate knowing there is laundry to fold, wine to pour, dishes to wash, your cock to suck, beds to make, and that I don't get to do any of it. There's that petulance again.

Here's what I propose if we continue emailing as friends: I'd love for it to be as lacking in pressure as possible.

I will temper my urge to write long emails often.

I will continue to be as patient as possible in waiting for a response.

But I won't promise not to interrupt the wait when it feels unmanageable. (I've always likened this to your instruction when scening that I was to let you know if the kneeling was too much.)

Please send tidbits along the way like you've done recently, or of course send good responses at any time.

And I hope you'll show up in and enjoy these interactions. If it's just going to be a drag for you, I'm hesitant to participate.

As ever, I wish you well.

I agree with your top three as some of the best bits of play we shared.

# WHAT DOES HE MEAN?

If I am cool and interesting, why can't we spend time together? If he wants to be my friend, what does he really mean by that – uninspired, lukewarm email? I want to be friends who see each other, who play cards together with other friends, share a meal or drinks every now and again, exchange ideas, enjoy each other's company. I want to actually know each other, not to have known each other.

And what does 'not in the foreseeable future mean'? If he means never see each other again, will he really tell me that? Is this to let me down easy? Will there come a time when he is willing, interested, and available to meet up?

# TOO LATE

For the last several months, so much in my relationship with Tracey was a test of some sort. When I asked how she was doing her answer was often, "Not very good and I don't want to talk to about it." When I asked more direct questions about her safety, whether she was at risk of hurting herself, whether she had a plan and the means, she shut down the conversation, refusing to answer my questions.

This was delicate territory as the younger sister with twelve years and five siblings between us, and as a licensed mental health therapist with my own clinical practice. I had to choose either to back off from that line of questioning to keep her as close to me as I could, or risk pushing her even further away by not respecting her boundaries. I mostly chose to back away.

Until she found her own way out.

Five weeks after we played dress up in preparation for my conference my sister ended her life on a lonely Wednesday in March. Our other sister and I found her the next day, dead in her apartment. It was a Thursday, my day to be in contact with her. She planned it that way, I know she did.

Tracey had a check-in call every day with one of her seven siblings. This plan was in place for years, as part of the discharge plan from her last stint on an inpatient psych ward. It changed the structure of our sibling connections forever. Tracey was the hub, connected to each of her siblings in ways none of the rest of us are with each other.

I rarely went more than a day without talking or texting with her and I definitely never missed my Thursday. Often, I'd pre-empt her calling me, because it's who I am, and because I'm hard to reach at work. That week, I saw her on Monday and called her Wednesday morning just to say hi. She didn't return my call, which wasn't all that unusual since it wasn't my day.

I started calling her Thursday morning, left messages on her voice mail at 9 am and noon. No return call, no text to say she got my messages. At 8 that evening, when I still hadn't heard from her, concern took over. Texts with our other sister told me she hadn't been in touch with Tracey that day either. We checked with our brothers to piece together who had talked with her and when. It didn't feel right. I felt a churning in the pit of my stomach and my fear took root.

Tracey knew when I didn't reach her that I'd go looking for her. She might not have known that Beth would be with me, but she knew I would come for her. And she knew it would be too late.

# OCTOPUS

When I finally returned home Thursday night, just past two in the morning, Summer was dozing on the futon in my living room. I opened the door and she jumped up to wrap her arms around me. I let go after just a few seconds, too hollow from shock to feel her support.

Flopping down on the recliner—exhausted but wired—I told Summer the next day's schedule as I knew it: sleep for a few hours, eat something, call extended family members and friends to break the news, meet at my parents' house in the evening to plan the funeral. In a numb fog, I brush my teeth and put myself to bed.

The next morning, I wake up early. I'm sad and disoriented. It doesn't feel real that she is gone. I know it is, I saw her dead body. Dead sister. I have a dead sister. She died. She's gone. She's never coming back to me. Panic rises in me. It seems I can push and pull it like a yo-yo, tossing it away from me before yanking it back by the string.

In those first few days, Summer never left my side. We joked that together we were an octopus – four arms, four legs, the equivalent of one brain: mine numb with disbelief and hers overloaded with worry.

We went to the greasy spoon breakfast joint in my neighborhood. Part of Summer's job was to make sure I ate. Our meal kept getting interrupted as friends who hadn't answered the night before started waking up to find that I'd called or texted. I broke the news to my inner circle on call after call in the vestibule of the Overlook restaurant. It was ok, I was still numb and therefore pretty calm.

After breakfast we went home to find phone numbers for more of my cousins. It felt strange to call relatives I've never spoken to by phone before, but we wanted to reach as many people as we could in the family, so no relatives found out from Facebook the next day.

# BACK AND FORTH

It wasn't a good idea. But that wasn't going to stop me. Still, I waited.

I had to reconcile myself to the possibility that he would say no. I wasn't allowed to ask if I couldn't handle him refusing. This is the deal I struck with myself. The early days of grief are all about making deals and staying busy.

Around lunchtime on Friday I tossed my idea out to Summer in one of the countless times she asked what I needed. "I think I want to ask Mr. Lucky if he'll let me come over," I said, like it wasn't ridiculous. She was giving me lots of leeway so her reply was kinder than it could have been. Mr. Lucky wasn't popular with her; she didn't approve of the way he treated me.

"Ok, what do you think he'll say?" Even in my compromised state, I could feel her small frame and fiery protective temper grasping for a gracious response.

"I don't know, probably no. I have to try. I just want him to hold me while I cry. He's done that before."

She didn't answer, just pulled her curly brown hair up into a bun, secured it with a pencil. I think she was hoping I'd realize on my own that this plan was ill-fated. We bantered about it throughout the day, between phone calls where I shared the news of my sister's death over and over. Summer held to her belief that reaching out to Mr. Lucky was a horrible idea, but said she'd support me if I chose to do it anyway.

I waited until late afternoon on Saturday to contact him. After an emergency session with my therapist and another night of fitful sleep. I waited as long as I could before reaching out for what I wanted most – the feel of Mr. Lucky's strong arms around me, holding me as I cried.

Our email correspondence was at a standstill again, with me waiting on him to reply as usual. I needed this ask to happen in a different context, so I sent a text, even though I knew he hated texting.

*Hi, it's Meg. I am reaching out as a friend, this is not about you and me. My sister just died and I am raw and seeking support. I am looking for a chance to cry and be held, for emotional release (not physical release) with someone who feels safe and comforting. Is that something you would be available for?*

His response arrived via email later that afternoon.

*hey meg. so sorry to hear about your sister. you have my condolences. today is fully booked, but if you want to talk tomorrow i could do that. i would prefer it be in a park, or coffee-shop or such.*

I read Summer his reply then drafted mine.

*Thank you for your words. What I want is the opportunity to sit on a couch together, cry and be held, which doesn't match with a park or coffee shop. I'm not sure my grief is fit for public consumption currently. I couldn't decipher your motivation for a public meeting place. One possible option is a private yet neutral space such as my office or the office of a friend. Thoughts?*

The next email from him contained only the question: *Where is your office located?*

Now I was irritated. I bitched to Summer, who was brushing her teeth down the hall from my desk. "What, is his Google broken? He knows where my office is…" I sent back just the address of my office.

Summer went to bed, leaving me at my desk trying to write, which mostly meant staring at the turquoise wall above the white frame of my desk, waiting for the next email from Mr. Lucky.

His response arrived: *is there a time that's good for you? earlier in the day is best for me.*

I replied with when I was free the next day, and then called out the unspoken discomfort in our exchange by asking. *Is this something that actually works for you?*

Eight minutes later, he answered. *it doesn't work naturally for me, since i don't see it as a role I should inhabit in your life. but i want to respect your grief and I don't know what other resources you have available.*

Irritation got pummeled by furious. I assured him that I had other support, then explained why I wanted him.

*I feel safe with you and have been physically close to you, and it was soothing and comforting. Also, having a chance to process around someone who is not also grieving the same loss is helpful. My brothers' arms bring comfort too, but we are in the same pool of grief.*

*My view is that if we're friends who intend to continue to know each other, this is a role you could inhabit in my life, and that I would want to be in for you if ever necessary. (I don't imagine you'd allow that, but it's something I would absolutely do for a friend.) But my feeling that you could doesn't make it right or appropriate if you don't want to be that kind of support to me.*

*Too many words…what I mean is: if it doesn't work for you, Mr. Lucky, that's okay with me. I'd rather hear the clear, honest truth than any answer you want to give to avoid hurting me. (If that is your motivation.)*

*If we do meet up, noon works for me. Is my office the place that feels acceptable to you?*

His next email held the answer that I realized was true all along.

*yeah, that's totally my motivation. i never want to hurt anyone but then i seem to stride around snubbing and disappointing people right and left somehow…*

*i am deeply glad to hear that you have resources to help you process your grief, and i want you to know that i continue to extend my warm regard for you personally and my sorrow at your loss, which i cannot realistically imagine. i'm thinking of the video clip you sent me on empathy, and how it's important to acknowledge the bruised feelings of people you want to support, without trying to swiftly correct them.*

*but your questions make it clear to me that right now i don't want to provide support in a hugging-on-a-couch way, so i don't think we should meet at your office. another time in a different context perhaps.*

*i'm sorry it took me so long to get to a clear and honest answer... it's not my strength. maybe in a way this brisk e-chatting can be my little support contribution.*

My reply was kinder than I felt. I wanted to encourage his expression of honesty, even though it took him so damn long. Because I'm an emotional masochist at least as much as a physical one, I asked if he was still willing to meet the next day to talk, in public.

*I appreciate you sticking with this exchange in order to get to your honest answer. Thank you for the regards and the expression of sorrow.*

*Would you still meet at a coffee shop to talk, or is that also truly outside of what works for you?*

*It's late, I don't need an answer tonight. You could let me know in the morning. I will be in SE for breakfast and it would be easy for me to meet at noon close to your house if that is something that works for you. Conversation and connection, minus the crying in your arms part, would still feel good to me if you are up for it. And if you're not, again, tell me clearly please.*

*It was a brisk back and forth, wasn't it? That's so unlike us.*

The next morning, ten minutes before we might have met up, in another email, he said no.

*Sun, Mar 16, 2014 at 11:50 AM*
*it takes so long sometimes for me to get to that honest answer!*

*i think meeting to talk is also outside of what works, which is hard for me to say. i'd like to keep things virtual or*

*whatever the right adjective is. But i'm willing to keep up
the brisk(ish) exchange throughout today and hear you
write about your sister, if that works for you.*

*(after i finish waking up. i stayed up much later than usual
trying to hang in with the briskness.)*

Sun, Mar 16, 2014 at 1:36 PM
How long it takes makes me appreciate your stick-to-it-ive-ness
even more, it feels respectful and kind.

Thank you for saying the hard thing. I really needed that. Will
you ever explain your desire to only interact via email? I needed a
different venue than our usual email back and forth to
communicate the news and my desire for support. I know you
don't like texting. I didn't forget that or disregard it out of
disrespect.

Thank you for the offer to continue communicating and to listen.
Thank you for staying up past your bedtime. I appreciate it.

More soon. Hope your Sunday is going well.

*Sun, Mar 16, 2014 at 1:59 PM
i've been thinking about empathy and how to helpfully
reply to people's needs without working too hard (i.e. to the
detriment of my own needs) to solve their problem for them.
in many cases, it seems, less is more.*

*your text sure got my attention (as soon as i noticed it!)
because i'm not a frequent texter or receiver of same, i
assume that any text i receive is super urgent...i didn't feel
beleaguered - mainly just worried.*

*i look forward to hearing what's on your mind.*

*also, thanks for respecting my desire to keep our communications in this form.*

Sun, Mar 16, 2014 at 2:53 PM
I like knowing you weren't bothered, just worried. Getting your attention was the point.

You are welcome for respecting your desire for email only. I look forward to you respecting mine for an answer about your need.

Right this minute, what's on my mind is how hard it was to tell my seven-year-old that her aunt just died. It's challenging to answer her questions honestly without saying too much, and difficult to field her random questions and segues. Her questions included: when did she die? will there be a funeral? did she die at the hospital or at her house or in her bed? how did she die? (followed by something else quickly enough that I got to evade that question—a huge relief—because how she died was suicide and I am reluctant to explain that part). She smiled a lot, told us not to worry because she would help us feel better. Then the ultimate segue: "I know, let's go play baseball, because all three of us are here now so we can have a pitcher and a catcher and a batter. That will help you feel better, Mom!"

I was really afraid to tell her. For as much as I value open, transparent communication, doing that as a parent of a verbally precocious child with emotional regulation challenges is a tall order.

But we did play baseball for a short bit. Not at all what I expected.

I might write more later about the narrative of what happened, as I haven't written it yet, just told it out loud.

*Sun, Mar 16, 2014 at 4:07 PM*
*at least partially it's that i don't want to mislead you into a deeper connection than i'm willing to support. one honest reaction to your text was me? why is she reaching out to me for this? shouldn't there be a lot of people further up that list?*

*her reactions sound a lot like I imagine seven year olds respond randomly to everything. the baseball thing is hilarious.*

*is this the first sibling you've lost? do you want to tell me about your reaction to the news?*

Sun, Mar 16, 2014 at 11:38 PM
I'm too tired to fully respond but want to thank you for your attention and thoughtful questions today. I'm grateful for your support in the way that worked for you. Getting a chance to write some of this out was helpful. I likely will return to your questions tomorrow and write more of the story.

Thank you for staying present and responding quickly.

More soon, but I know that the work week starts tomorrow for you and I don't expect the same quick turnaround as last night or today.

*Mon, Mar 17, 2014 at 12:39 AM*
*please do send more of the story. i feel like i've only heard*
*how you are dealing with the tragedy in your life, and not*
*how it's made you feel.*


Mon, Mar 17, 2014 at 8:23 PM
I use so many words to get to my own clarity. (You've noticed.) I
do it out loud too, but writing accesses a different part of my
brain. Knowing I am understood or that what I'm saying makes
sense has always been paramount to me. My worthiness and
acceptability are all tangled up in there.

I always want your honest reaction, and I understand why you
questioned my reaching out to you. It's incredibly challenging to
allow myself to cry and receive physical comfort. I crave it yet
don't let myself ask for or receive it. There are very few people
I'm willing to go there with who also meet these criteria: they are
male, they are bigger than me so I can feel small in their arms, I
feel safe with them emotionally and physically. You're on that list
because of the intimacy we've shared in play, because I trust you
and the ways you have demonstrated attunement in our
connection. I am surrounded by people I can talk to who love
and support me. But hardly any of them meet my criteria for
crying my heart out in their arms.

It's interesting to wonder how each of us defines a deep
connection. I do friendship deep, I just do. And writing is one of
my most intimate ways to connect. When we're both present in
it, I find our correspondence very intimate. I don't think we
mean the same thing when we say we want to be friends. I'd like a
chance to converse with you about that sometime or at least read
your thoughts on it.

Yeah, the baseball thing was something else. She'd had enough
serious talk and needed to break the mood. She's smart enough to

know that doing something physical moves emotion through her system. I can relate.

I just found a piece of writing from over a decade ago about play as catharsis that feels so contemporary it's eerie. It applies even more now with this loss. I'll share it if you want to read it.

This is the first sibling I've lost. Heather was like a sister to me but this is different. Tracey was my oldest sister. She was twelve years my senior, and my closest family member, the one who has most consistently truly seen me.

And the thing is, I didn't hear the news. I discovered it. My other sister and I are the ones who found her.

My feelings are such a convoluted mix. I'm sad, angry, hurt, relieved. I am grateful to not be confused. There isn't any question about why she did it, she just couldn't keep pushing anymore. She couldn't get out from the sadness; it was just too big. We told our daughter that Tracey's brain was sick and she had a sadness bigger than the ocean that didn't get better. We explained how it's different than the sad that people often feel— sad the size of rain drops or a puddle—that kind of sad gets better and we feel other things like happy too.

This is long so I am going to stop here for now.


*Tue, Mar 18, 2014 at 1:04 PM*
*in my experience you use a lot of your verbal efforts to solicit others to talk and to clarify their own processing.*

*good explanation of why you reached out to me. i see how you got there, and feel more logical understanding of the situation.*

*yeah, clearly the staying-in-contact situation needs to be synchronized. i do friendship deep, but in my own way, part of which entails fighting off any non-self-driven obligation. i think i'm getting to a point of explaining my friendship views in our other thread...*

*ah. that's an interesting thing! it could well be a bad habit, to seek to break the mood too soon (or I suppose too late, although that's never been my problem) but it's also so necessary to know enough's enough - and to balance your personal enough against the needs of your co-talkers.*

*please do share that writing.*

*i'm doubly sorry that you lost your closest family member, knowing that you sometimes struggle to connect with your family.*

*no one's strength is limitless, it seems. what makes you angry?*

Tue, Mar 18, 2014 at 1:11 PM
Here's that piece of writing I mentioned [written to/about Sheldon way back when]:

I just want you to fuck me – order me around, let me challenge you but lose, want me enough that sometimes you let your guard down. Trust me – respect my limits after testing them soundly. And fuck me. Tell me I'm a sexy whore you can't resist. Punish me for making you want me. Fuck me anywhere you choose. I'll do what you say. Strip me naked and make me show off for you. Tease me with your hard cock – taunt me knowing that's what I want more than anything. Bind my arms and legs so I can struggle against you. Let me swear at you as you use me. Embrace my anger and feed it back to me. Choke me with your cock until I gasp, pant, beg you to stop. Slap my face hard and slander me for getting wet. Lay me on my back to get myself off in front of you. Listen to me talk dirty about your cock, my need, how hungry I am for you. Push me to the point of begging for mercy. Let me beg. Push me harder until I really beg, until I no longer believe in mercy, until I've really given myself to you. Then fuck me hard and caress me with praise. Accept my tears and don't ask me why they're here. Hold me close, let me fight myself, let me purge this fear, this anger, this grief. Then send me home – a kiss on my forehead, a swat at my ass as I walk away, broken and whole, terrified and safe, free to live.

Tue, Mar 18, 2014 at 10:32 PM
Does how I invite you to clarify your processing feel different in our written connection than verbally? Do you experience it as annoying or pushy?

I'm excited to read the explanation you come up with (said with no pressure). I'm afraid my saying I do friendship deep somehow implied that you don't. Not my intention at all.

Yes, essential to find the balance of needs. I imagine our fill lines for talking are pretty divergent. Anything else I say here could sound clinical and I don't want to go there.

What surprised me in that writing was how it could have been written to you. Also, I left this part out when I sent it:

...I don't think I can do that with anyone I love. I can't show that part of me to anyone who has any other place in my life. Am I ashamed of it? Terrified to admit it exists? Scared I won't come back from it? Yes...and no. I don't need that release all the time. And I haven't had it since Heather died. There is a way that bottoming brings me to a place emotionally that I can't get to any other way. Or I don't want to get to any other way. I could get there emotionally – I'd hate it…fidgeting and caving in on myself, not wanting anyone near me, angry at not finding the words I need, unsure of how to get gracefully out of this predicament – how to tuck all those loose threads of chaos back into their secure hiding spot until I melt down again. If it's a scene, it's over the minute I walk out the door…

Much of that part has changed - I am more adept at verbally processing emotions now. I can imagine doing kink with someone I love. And I'm not ashamed of it.

The things you remember and reflect back to me are touching. I feel seen and that feels good. Thank you.

I'm angry that none of us could make it better enough that my sister could stay. I know it wasn't up to us to save her. And I'm angry at how much planning she did, and that my intuition didn't arrive in time to intervene. Again, I know it wasn't my job and I truly don't blame myself. But that's where anger comes in. I'm angry that this is the third suicide my family is weathering.

Thank you for your attention and support through this exchange, Mr. Lucky. It means a lot. I don't feel urgency about responses and definitely don't want you to feel obligated to continue. This is much more contact than you've had with me lately and while I appreciate it, I don't expect it of you. Especially since it sounds like you are also working on our other thread. Please show up here when and how it works for you. Having a place to send some writing has been helpful.

# BIRTHDAY PARTY

I built my birthday girl outfit around a pair of fabulous orange wedge-heeled sandals. They had been Tracey's – one of thirty pairs of shoes I inherited from her. The dress was hers too, found in her closet, new with tags. The white sundress with small polka dots in pink, orange, and grey looked like me, so I kept it. The shoes added four inches to my height. I would always be the youngest in the family but for one night I wasn't also the shortest.

My 40th birthday party was planned before my sister died. Two weeks before the party, I broke down in therapy. "I don't want my own birthday to be like all the other family events," I complained to Gayle. "I go into them eager for real connection and leave dejected, feeling lonely and unseen." Gayle urged me to revamp the celebration.

"I know your family loves you," she reflected. "But they often don't show it in ways that resonate with you." She knew from a decade of working together that this event wasn't likely to be any different.

I pressed on, stubborn and hopeful, true to my Taurus nature. My sister Beth agreed to host the party and together we planned the menu: a taco bar, chocolate cupcakes, fresh fruit and vanilla ice cream. My brothers offered to chip in for the food and I let them.

The finishing touch of my outfit was a corsage I made out of the ribbons from last year's birthday gifts from Tracey. The colorful curls of fabric swirled above my heart. It was the best way to imagine her close to me. There were moments when the pang of missing her stung, when the memories of last year's birthday beach adventure sliced through me.

I arrived early to help Beth set up, anxious for something to do. Offering to help is a path to belonging in my family. If I am useful, I can feel included. It's just one of the ways my family life preordained my desire for submission. I was raised to be pliant, obedient, useful, and polite.

Fussing about in Beth's kitchen before the party guests arrived calmed me down. I set out paper plates and napkins decorated with stars. She caught my eye across the table we were setting together. "I know you miss her. She should be here." She stopped talking and blinked back tears. My eyes welled up, too. Tracey's absence was the elephant in the room. I appreciated Beth not shying away from what we both felt.

As birthday parties go, it was fun. Everyone loved the tacos and dessert was delicious. A chorus of relatives sang an out of tune Happy Birthday as I blew out candles shaped like a four and a zero on my cupcake.

The only thing I wished for was impossible, but I closed my eyes and wished for her anyway.

# ECHOES

There are echoes, reverberations of all the things I want to say but don't, memories of things I said and wish I hadn't.

I remember the times I laid myself bare to him, shivering in anticipation of his touch and warm on the inside from the swell of my own desire. Was it always that way – the rush of hot intensity from me meeting the slow freeze of his cool demeanor? Detached, distant, cold, calculating. Even his passion is temperate, reserved.

I am working to disengage from him, to unhook myself from wanting to see and be seen there. His lack of presence has become a full-blown absence, nestled into place among the other losses I've endured. Some ancient, some freshly carved into my heart.

*Tue, May 13, 2014 at 6:55 AM*
*I'm amalgamating two half-written emails to you (below), in an effort to demonstrate my interest in staying in contact and in clearly defining the parameters of that contact. And to clear out the draft folder, which makes me tense.*

*email draft 1:*
*I haven't been great at communicating what I'm available*

*for, and I doubt I'll be much better if I wait, so here it is in breakdown form, which I think you might have sympathy with as my analogue to your silly surveys:*

*In-person meetings: none for now*
*Play: none in person for now*
*Email frequency: low*
*Email intensity: medium*
*Email submissiveness: light but noticeable*
*Memories: pleasant and not wistful*
*Erotic picture attachments: when appropriate*

*email draft 2:*
*i won't be quick to throw our connection away in any case: it's not often one meets a cock worshipper with your devotion. cheers to that!*

*i propose we keep chatting over email for now and for the foreseeable future. that's all i've got. i'll try to keep up a regular communication (read: weekly at least) and you try to not beleaguer me with too much text, too many questions, or too much attachment.*
*// end draft emails*

*I'm intentionally not editing those.*

*Tell me what's going on with you?*

# TARGET

When I go to Target I usually have a list of one or two items that necessitated the trip. But then the wandering kicks in and I discover more things I must have. Driving today, poring over Mr. Lucky's email in my head, I cracked myself up with this Target shopping analogy. Yes, he sought one thing out of our connection and he got that in spades. What he didn't anticipate and rarely acknowledges are the extras he appreciates about me that he didn't go looking for.

When the ball rests in my court my anxiety mews quietly instead of growling with intensity. I can let myself rankle where his words irritate me and determine how I want to respond. And I can savor the words that show where he's willing to be present.


Sat, May 17, 2014 at 12:04 AM
I appreciate this demonstration of your interest in staying in contact. You know there's a cure for those pesky draft folders...

Is this *for now* business just a placeholder or do you actually intend to see me and or play in person at some point? I remain confused (albeit more calmly) by your unwillingness to meet up.

The emails I sent prior to my sister's funeral clearly exceeded your intensity threshold as they never got a response. I can imagine not knowing how to reply to such raw content.

Abiding by your stated parameters seems to meet the submissiveness quotient.

It's good to know what motivates you to keep me around. My cock worshipping devotion is of little benefit to either of us when we aren't seeing each other in person.

The idea of regular communication from you is a fair compromise to your expectation that I trim the quantity of text I send and limit my questions. I do wonder why it matters how many questions I send - you answer them selectively anyway.

I wish I could map the edges of this foreseeable future and track the relevant variables. My attachment has been appropriately pruned and continues to wither of its own accord.

Grief is exhausting and distracting. It takes an enormous toll on my work, my body, and my general attentiveness to detail. I miss my sister intensely.

Tell me what's going on with you, please. How are things in your relationship? [Am I allowed to ask that?] Are the calla lilies in your yard blooming?

# WRITING WORKSHOP

I taught a writing workshop today using song lyrics as prompts. For each timed write I handed out the lyrics to a song and we listened together. Then we wrote for ten to twelve minutes — maybe related to the song prompt, maybe not, and took turns reading those fresh words out loud.

*Angry Anymore — by Ani Difranco.* I just want you to understand that I didn't see this coming. I just want you to understand that falling in love with you was an accident. It wasn't my intention. And it wasn't all my doing. You switch your attunement off and on at will, sometimes present and responsive, but more often distant and aloof. This intermittent schedule of attention from you doesn't help.

Every time I think you're done, that you've finally decided to leave for good, you write me again and state your desire to remain in contact. You drop casual placeholders, say in-person connection is unavailable for now, and cite an ambiguous foreseeable future. But I can't see this future you envision. You joke about why you keep me around, and part of me thinks it's funny but the rest of me is hurt and incredulous.

I just want you to understand that I tried not to fall in love with you. I tried to tamp down the obsession before it took hold. But it didn't work. Maybe if you had only been aloof and distant or if we had kept our connection to the limited parameters we first laid out, it might have worked. But you created intimacy and emotional attachment too, that wasn't just me. You reached past your own limits to engage with me and then drew yourself away like a hand from a hot stove. You felt it. I know you did.

I just want you to understand that I don't regret falling in love with you.

*February – by Dar Williams.* You fashioned the key to my heart out of words – volleyed back and forth, quick-witted and clever. You openly shared your own desires when you could have hidden behind your role in this exchange. Early on, I focused the beam of my attention on you, drew you out with thoughtful, compelling questions. This is who I am and what I do – an occupational mixed blessing. You relished the opportunity to tell me who you are – until you didn't anymore. Until my interest in you felt like an attempt to subsume you.

Your touch lit up my body with sensations I'd been away from too long. But your words composed overlapping melodies in my heart and mind. I believe you know that your words leak the truth of your emotions, which is why you stay disconnected in our writing. Is that why you take weeks to respond and even then, send only fragments? I used words to gain access to you, too. Choosing carefully, I balanced my language with enough deference to be appropriate and sufficient challenge to keep you interested. I miss your touch, your firm hands, strong chest, scruffy face. But your words will always hold the key to me.

# GROUNDING

I don't understand what's going on with Mr. Lucky and I'm starting to think he's purposefully being an ass. His absence never seemed calculated or malicious before, but now I'm not sure. He proposed being in touch at least weekly and now eleven days have gone by with no response from him.

I long to scene with him again, crave that verbal and physical roughness and the opportunity to please him. I want to ground in my body through that physical intensity, sexual tension, and release.

# CHALLENGE

I could do it. His number is right there in my phone, filed under his actual name.

My heart would beat an insistent staccato as the call connects. The suspense of the ringing would taste sour on my tongue. Would he pick up? Is my number saved in his phone? It must be, under my first name I'd guess. Does he have nicknames for me that I'll never know?

The ringing would interrupt my wondering...

I'd hear the abrupt end of a ring and then his voice, the one I haven't heard in almost six months. "Why are you calling me?" No hello, no curt greeting, just a challenge from the outset.

"Hi..." I would stammer.

"What do you want?" Yes, that's the voice I've missed, that accent from the heartland with the perpetual hint of a wry smirk.

"I just want to know how you are, what's going on with you."

"You've taken pre-empting my email to a new level." He wouldn't sound amused. "I'm planning to write you. Unfinished attempts lurk in my drafts folder."

"I'm done waiting for emails. It isn't working. I want answers. Even when you do reply you evade my questions." This bold language wouldn't match how scared I'd feel. "Please, just talk to me, or tell me, finally, why you won't."

*Tue, Jun 10, 2014 at 10:26 PM*
*Greetings! I hope late spring/early summer is treating you well. I'm in pretty good shape but insanely busy. All my friends emerged from hibernation with a taste for socializing.*

*The big news is that a good friend of mine is moving into my house...times are hard for him and it feels good to offer him a place of refuge.*

*I hear your confusion. For now is legit, although it's far more likely that I will want to/be able to hang out platonically than in a play setting in the foreseeable. My sexual situation is complicated and, before you ask, I really don't have a good enough handle on it to define it.*

*Indeed, those emails you sent were intense. Don't think they aren't lurking in my Draft folder. Please know that I read and absorbed them.*

*The calla lilies, which were despaired of after the cold, are blooming nicely. My relationship, which was despaired of after the cold, remains in a functional limbo. Big changes on the horizon will probably cause it to settle into a less fluid state, more capable of satisfying definition. Things are okay.*

*I thought of you a lot the past few weeks, perhaps because I was up around your neighborhood several times. Never with any unscheduled time available, but someday I'll probably text you a mind-if-i-drop-in note. Let me know if that's not okay.*

# SNARK FEST

Tonight's email from Mr. Lucky evokes so much anger, hurt, and general what-the-fuck-itude that I just have to write my way through it. These are the outraged, incredulous, snide responses that I won't be sharing with him.

Oh, how fucking charming that you can offer your good friend refuge. Thanks for sharing that, seeing as how when my sister died suddenly and I asked you for help, you said no. No, you didn't want to support me in that crying on the couch sort of way. And no, you wouldn't meet up and talk in a cafe, even though that was your initial counteroffer. I can guess at all sorts of reasons why it's different with this good friend than with me. But it still fucking hurts. And you are either a complete asshole to rub my nose in this or you're merely oblivious, which is also maddening.

Please don't bother responding to the emails about my sister's death at this point. What the fuck could you possibly say now, almost three months later?

Thanks for being so goddamn vague about things in your relationship.

Seriously?! I haven't seen you in six months because you're unwilling to meet in person, and now you want to know if you can drop in sometime? And you text now?

Sat, Jun 21, 2014 at 8:50 AM
Thanks for sharing bits of what you're busy with these days.

Your friend is a lucky chap - your home and your company are a fine sanctuary indeed.

I felt a sharp twinge of hurt at your reference to offering refuge to your friend since you weren't willing to support me in the physically present way I asked of you when my sister died. Likely that speaks to differing levels of commitment, engagement, and connection in that friendship compared to whatever this is we've constructed out of typed characters exchanged in the ether. (We both refer to it as friendship, but this is unlike any friendship I've ever known.) Nonetheless, it stung, which I tell you solely for the purpose of speaking the truth about my experience.

Well, at least you can anticipate my question-asking habits by now. Fair enough. What I gather is: there is a sexual situation; it doesn't currently include me; you are reticent to talk about it. That's all been consistently true for a good six months now. I'm open to it changing but not holding any expectation that it will.

Hopefully the changes in your relationship will bring you more of what you want. I'm glad to hear the calla lilies are thriving.

You've been in my thoughts recently, too. I'm open to a *can-i-drop-by* text. It might shock me to receive non-email contact from you, but I'll manage. I'd also like to make concrete plans to see you. It's hard to pin anything on someday probably - which is possibly your point. Here are some ideas:

I'm reading again soon, most likely a piece or two from my book-in-progress. Want to come listen?

Tom Petty and the Heartbreakers concert at the Moda Center Tuesday, August 12th? I tried to get at least one of my brothers to go with me and they all declined.

There's always that game of dominoes we haven't played yet. Brunch, dinner, or drinks out? Let me know what you're up for and when you are free. This friend of yours has a taste for socializing too.

# AN UNSENT PROPOSITION

I don't know about you, but I could use the catharsis of a good scene. I want to feel the impact of a hand slapping my face and my tits, fingers teasing my cunt, the sting of a belt against my bare ass. I crave the smooth leather of a collar buckled in place to mark me as someone's property for the moment.

I could use being someone's bitch for an evening, a cock whore heeding her Sir's commands in hopes that she'll get the sweet reward of swallowing his load of cum.

You have set the limit of no in person play, for now - for that goddamned foreseeable future that I want to scream at every time you use that phrase. The future I want has me on my knees in front of you in whatever state of undress you've commanded, hands behind my back, dropping us both back into our dynamic with our scene opening ritual.

Do you want it too? Do you want to use me as your slut for a lunch hour or an evening? Do you have any laundry to fold or dishes to wash or just want to boss me around?

I want it. I want to feel alive in my body, to connect with my own flesh and emotions in the way only submission creates in me. I want it because I miss you and the play we did. I want it because grief and overwhelm and fear and longing are heavy to carry around all the damn time and I need a break. I want to lose myself in the freedom of being owned.

So, Sir, are you game?

I can anticipate your answer, taste the chalky, bitter *no* of your likely response. It would hurt to be rejected flat out, but it might also be a relief to hear what I imagine is true. I'd like to hear you own up to the truth that you don't want me, or somehow convince me that your desire remains, but some other variable is an obstacle.

In November, when I spoke of seeking similar emotional release through submission, you said that as my friend you'd do anything you could to support me. Clearly that isn't still the case, which makes asking you this feel reckless. But here I am, asking anyway. What do I have to lose by being this forward? You always said there was nothing wrong with the play we did. We agreed on that.

So, do you want me? And please do me the favor of not taking three weeks to respond to this.

# LAG TIME

I play an interactive word game with a few friends, taking turns back and forth in the app on our phones. It amuses me that this app nudges me when I haven't taken my turn. Notifications read *It's been 3 days!* since a word was played. I often have this same reaction to Mr. Lucky's slow response time. I've been known to open my Gmail inbox, search for our current thread and count how many days I've been waiting for him to write back. I report this number to myself with the same urgent punctuation as the word game app. *It's been 16 days!* (non-random example of current lag time).

I'm untangling myself from this connection with Mr. Lucky. He's seeking casual sex partners from a new dating profile and I'm angry at him for not communicating honestly with me, again (still).

I do want to play with him again to release the emotions lodged in my body. But I know better than to send him that proposition. I'm pretty sure that window has passed now – he's no longer a safe play partner for me. Right now I'm more likely to call and give him a piece of my mind.

# TEMPER TANTRUM

Last week's session with my therapist was unusual. It was the day of my dad's gallbladder surgery and I was wrung out from worry. Minutes before my session with Gayle, I heard that dad came through surgery fine, but it hadn't sunk in yet.

I sat on the floor of Gayle's office in my usual spot at her feet and cried in her lap for a few minutes. When I could speak again, I told her I was overwhelmed by my dad's health crisis. And then, of course, there's Mr. Lucky who is totally absent, isn't keeping his end of the staying in touch bargain and refuses to explain why he won't see me.

"I don't know how to move all of this emotion through my body," I vent to Gayle. "I just want to kick and scream, to throw a temper tantrum!"

"Great," she smiles. "Let's do it! Stand up!" She steps away briefly and returns with a dishtowel, tossing one end to me. Once it lands in my grip I come alive; I yank us into a game of tug of war.

She pretends to be Mr. Lucky and I let loose. "You fucking ass, what's so complicated about your sexual situation that you can't tell me you're looking for casual sex with other people? Did you really think your photo wouldn't show up in my dating app feed? Why don't you tell me the fucking truth?" I pull and fight and scream and kick until I'm spent. I drop the towel and fold myself into Gayle's soothing embrace. We stand together and she holds me as I cry.

Emotion pulses through me as I erupt within this permission to be angry at Mr. Lucky, to want to read him the riot act or beat the shit out of him.

I leave Gayle's office feeling grounded in my body and so much calmer. Worries about my dad and the stress of care-taking both he and my mom this week still swarm around me, but I feel more equipped to step into that fray.

# RIDICULOUS

I just spent almost an hour staring at my phone trying to wrangle the courage to call Mr. Lucky. It's been three weeks of silence from him. I made a list of what I might say if he answered or I had to leave a voice mail. I wanted to sound as if I didn't have to prove to him why I was calling.

Along with staring at my phone, I poked around online, wrote a few emails, ate a snack, and emptied the trash at my office where I'm hanging out for the evening. But the whole time I was psyching myself up to push the damn button and dial his number.

Finally, I scolded myself for being ridiculous and I did it. I called him. I'm not sure I was breathing while his phone rang, and I wasn't surprised when it went to voice mail. His outgoing message is simple and direct, "This is Mr. Lucky, leave me a message." So I did.

"Hey Mr. Lucky, it's Meg. I'm working on what to read next week and I realized I wanted to know whether you'd be at my reading. I don't want to be surprised by you showing up; I've had enough surprises lately with running into your new dating profile. And I didn't want to send another email that wouldn't likely get a timely response. So I thought I'd call. I hope all the transitions going on for you are treating you well. I'll talk to you later."

There, I did it. I'm relieved that I stopped being chicken and made the call. I don't know if it will shift anything in him, but I needed to create my own movement from fear to courage.

*Thu, Jul 10, 2014 at 7:30 AM*
*I got your voice message, and I will not be attending the reading, so don't worry about surprises. I hope it goes great.*

*I'm increasingly aware that I have done a poor job giving you the support and connection that you're searching for. This is mainly because it's not the support and connection that I want to be giving, and I was foolish and unfair to leave that unclear and unexpressed. So I am ending our connection, and I apologize for not doing so sooner.*

*You have expressed that you are actively looking for a partner — I'm sure you'll find one and that it will be a positive development.*

*You're awesome and I wish you the best. Be well.*

# STICK FIGURE

Mr. Lucky was once again the main attraction in therapy today. In processing my initial response to his last email, I stumbled into an analogy that works for me. When I first met Mr. Lucky, I was fresh out of my marriage, just two months into living apart from my ex. I was the equivalent of a stick figure.

Throughout the last year, I've grown into a more fully fleshed out version of myself. As I became more embodied, I offered so much of myself to Mr. Lucky. Showing him this more expansive me was part of becoming my whole self. He didn't ignite or reawaken the writer or the sexually vibrant person in me; I did that. But it happened in the context of my submissive relationship with him.

Gayle described how submission originates from many places, including: feeling low, worthless, and disempowered; or conversely feeling grounded, powerful, and consciously loaning that power to another for the electricity it generates.

When I met Mr. Lucky, I was coming from that second place. The more he retreated from our connection, the more my energy sank into that first expression of submission.

The issue was not that I wasn't enough; if anything, I offered more than he wanted of what worked for him. I mattered to him. He refused to show it or offer any appreciation for it, but it's true. I know it is.

"Why do I want the last word with him?" I asked Gayle in session.

"I think you want external acknowledgement," she said, "and that you're claiming your power." Her warm smile made me shy; the depth of her awareness is both a comfort and an edge for me.

In an effort to manage my reactions to his email, I'm not allowing myself to do any of the following: 1) explore his social media page, which I visit regularly since discovering it nine months ago, and which I last checked the night I called him; 2) troll his dating profile; 3) obsessively re-read yesterday's email from him, or torture myself by reading back through any of our correspondence. There will be time enough for that; it isn't going anywhere.

# WHERE I STAND NOW

I've been all over the map since Thursday's email from Mr. Lucky. Rage, hurt, sadness, remorse, regret, longing, shame, relief. I've been tempted to storm the castle (my shorthand for showing up unannounced at his home to say goodbye in person), or to tell him off by phone or email. Today, for the first time, I realized that not responding at all is a viable option. I hadn't considered that.

Everyone but Gayle is adamant that showing up uninvited to see him is not wise. It occurred to me that Gayle appears to support me, not because she agrees that I should storm the castle, but to reinforce the idea that I can do whatever the fuck I want about this. I can feel and express whatever I'm feeling. Why wouldn't I have the last word?!

What's most clear is my desire for a different sort of closure with him. I've spent the day gently drafting an email to him in my head.


Thu, Jul 17, 2014 at 10:17 PM
I understand from your email that you are done being in contact with me and I intend to respect your need to end our connection. I'm just not quite there yet.

As you hopefully remember, my request about if/when you were done was that you would: 1) clearly tell me, which you did in your 'Update' email, for which I am grateful. (Horrible euphemism, though, that subject heading. That wasn't an update, that was an ending); 2) do so in person because it would devastate me to not get to say goodbye.

I would like you to honor the second part of my request and meet with me in person to say goodbye and complete our exchange. After that, you won't hear from me again unless we both wish it.

Consider it delayed aftercare to officially close our D/s dynamic. I offered you my submission in good faith that it would be respected and held appropriately. Not having one of very few specific requests honored feels like a significant breach of that trust.

Consider it penance for stringing me along for seven months.

Consider it common courtesy and decency.

Consider it an appropriate end to a largely successful series of interactions.

Consider it what you will, but please reach past your deflections and meet with me.

Although we measured the value of our interactions differently, we both found our exchanges potent. I don't want the end of this story to be that I feel hostility towards you for your unwillingness to meet with me. Having lived through two sudden deaths without the opportunity to say goodbye has been a defining experience in my life. Your exit from my life, while not in any way as dramatic, debilitating, or meaningful as those losses, does not need to be tossed onto that particular pyre.

I am purposely sending this to you in multiple venues because I want to be sure you see it. My plan is to email it, send it via a dating app message, and text you that I sent you a message. I'm counting on you to respond within a week so I'm not left hanging. Please don't let me down.

I feel certain that, in the long run, good closure for both of us is a much better outcome - one that honors the level of conscious consent in which our relationship was formed and will allow us both to walk away with mutual care and respect.

*Mon, Jul 21, 2014 at 8:36 PM*
*Sounds good. I will certainly enjoy seeing you again.*

*Naturally, scheduling is tough and may cause closure-delay. That said, how about meeting up on the morning of Sunday, August 3rd, at Peninsula Park in your neighborhood?*

# WHAT THE FUCK?

Just when I thought he might punk out for good, when I started to face the fact that he might be a bigger chump than I ever really thought possible, he writes me back. He's agreed to meet. This line of his short email threw me. *Sounds good. I will certainly enjoy seeing you again.*

Dude, seriously? You'll enjoy seeing me again to tell me goodbye forever because you don't want to give me the support and connection I'm looking for? What the fuck?

# EMPTY SOLACE

I've never made a date for the sole purpose of saying goodbye. How will I manage to dim the bright, wet longing for him that still swims in the freckles on my skin?

I can conjure within me a desire to be stoic, to offer a cold and calm farewell without letting him see the swath of destruction cut through me by his absence.

But I know myself. I understand that I will unfurl before him all nervous smiles and tender deference. Candor, not anger, will slip from my tongue – the tongue that once caressed his body with unrestrained hunger. I will offer too much of myself. Knowing it will be the last time is an empty solace.

I won't allow myself to hide within a hope that this isn't goodbye, that somehow in this brief public moment he will step forward again into the intensity of our connection, will meet me there to join, not disengage.

I will need to hold my heart back, curb her greedy longing in order to square my gaze with his and let him go.

Thu, Jul 31, 2014 at 8:59 PM
Is there any other possible outcome besides saying goodbye on
Sunday and dissolving our connection?

*Fri, Aug 1, 2014 at 11:29 AM*
*There's no other outcome I want right now. But I like you and I pretty much never want to do anything irrevocable. Let's save the issue for a face-to-face conversation, okay?*

*I'll see you at the park at 10 a.m.*

# FINDING MOLLY

I knew I wasn't done. Whether or not I'd play with Mr. Lucky again was out of my hands. But I needed to extricate myself from the feeling that I still belonged to him. I clung to the idea that I could have managed the ending better if I'd known it would be our last scene. But neither of us knew that night what the future might hold.

Weeks turned to months and his willingness to communicate with me evaporated, yet I couldn't shake the felt sense of being his. Even after he refused to support me when my sister died, I wanted him. I'd been tasked with carrying so much sadness, grief, rage, fear, confusion, and overwhelm. The relief I sought could only happen through my body. I needed rough physical and sexual input, harsh words, striking physical contact. I needed intensity dialed up to eleven.

Of course, I wanted to do this with Mr. Lucky. Our entire connection was built around kinky sex play; that's all it was ever supposed to be. But since I also had to purge emotional distress about him, he wouldn't have been a good fit.

Finding the right person was more difficult than I expected. I wanted to play with a man but didn't know any local male dominants. One man, a referral from my therapist Gayle, helped me clarify how I imagined the work unfolding, but decided not to step into the physicality of the play with me. When a friend involved in the local kink scene recommended a female friend of hers who does domme work, I decided to contact her.

The night I finally felt brave enough to email Molly I was on vacation sharing a summer rental with my parents, my daughter, and a handful of my siblings. After the kiddo was tucked into bed, I sat at the kitchen island and sent a brief request to this friend of my friend. There would be time for details – this was just an introduction.

When four days went by without a reply, I checked in with my friend, careful not to triangulate the connection. "Is it unusual for Molly to take this long to respond to an email?" She confirmed that it was unlike Molly and encouraged me to reach out again. I pushed past my fear and resent my message.

This time she replied in a couple of hours. Apparently my first inquiry never reached her. She was interested in my request but needed more information about the work I wanted to do. I explained:

*I want to submit to someone for physical and emotional catharsis. I am dealing with traumatic grief (my sister died by suicide four months ago) and also the painful loss of a Dom I was playing with who is no longer emotionally present or available to me. That relationship was truncated in a way that left me feeling stuck, and that, coupled with my sister's death, has me wanting to scene to get some of this emotional energy out in a physical, sexual way through submission. And unfortunately, I'm single and don't have any readily available partners to do this with, so I'm seeking someone outside my circle instead.*

Her initial concern was whether I could process my anger at Mr. Lucky with a female top. I admitted to wondering the same thing. It seemed feasible if the top had a strong enough presence to command the scene. I had a hunch she did.

After exchanging a few emails about what we might do together, we met in person to construct the details of our scene. Molly and I sat together on the red couch in my counseling office. In her low-cut black dress and sexy black sandals, she exuded warm confidence and calm compassion. She was beautiful and kind and I already felt safe in her presence. She was definitely the right choice for this. Nervousness flushed my cheeks and softened my voice. "I just want you to step into Mr. Lucky's role so I can rail against him and get rid of this rage and sadness."

I shared details about my dynamic with Mr. Lucky and agreed to send her a story I'd written about playing with him. She needed these contextual details to craft her role. We also discussed the boundaries and limits of our play. No kissing, and sexual contact would only happen from her to me.

Molly and I set a date for a Friday evening. I wanted to scene with her before I met Mr. Lucky in the park to say goodbye, but that timing didn't work out. Instead, we scheduled it at the end of my week, at the close of a moderately busy day, when I knew I'd be tired and more likely to fall apart emotionally. Catharsis was my goal after all.

With Mr. Lucky, my only input for our scenes was to show up at his house as instructed, thereby consenting to the things he had planned for us; but with Molly I got to co-create the interaction. From our emails and that conversation in my office we scripted a scene that would hopefully evoke the freedom I sought. Everything was set for me to arrive at her house-turned-dungeon Friday after work.

We agreed that I would call her Sir, the honorific I used with Mr. Lucky. It was fun for me to imagine this strong, red-haired femme Top presenting masculine for this scene. How would she pull it off?

More importantly, what the hell was I going to wear for this scene?

# SUNDAY IN THE PARK

"He's been like a ghost in my life all this time, affecting my days without actually being present. And now he'll just walk back into my line of sight. What the hell?" I'm in my car crying on the phone to Summer. She tries soothing me but it's pointless. There will be no calm in me until this meeting is over, maybe not even then.

I'm halfway into another plaintive rant when I spot him in the rose garden waiting for me. It takes a minute to recognize him in the outside world since we've only ever shared space at his house. "Shit, he's already here, I gotta go."

"You've got this. Call me after."

I dry my eyes, step out of the car, and walk toward him. He's in shorts and a sweatshirt with a backpack slung over one broad shoulder. The dark curls of his short hair are mostly contained under a baseball hat. He hears my footsteps, turns and smiles at me. That damned smile still creates earthquakes in my nervous system.

"Hello, Meg." It's an unqualified warm greeting.

"Hi, Mr. Lucky." He reaches to hug me and I notice a pint of blueberries in his hand.

"I figured it was my turn to bring the berries," he says. I melt a little at the reference. On our first date I brought him fresh raspberries as an offering. His thoughtfulness catches me off guard. I sink into his arms for a brief moment, determined not to get lost there.

Disentangling from his embrace, I locate my voice. "Let's find a place to sit. Maybe that bench?" I point to a spot still shaded from the Sunday morning sunshine. As we sit down I smooth my bright blue striped skirt across my lap, nervously tug at my purple t-shirt.

In my purse is a handful of colored index cards, notes I scribbled in case this is the last time I ever see him. At first it was just questions for him, but I forced myself to include things I wanted a chance to say.

*What exactly doesn't work for you in this connection? Why does it have to end?*

*I never wanted you to be someone I used to know.*

*Are you getting to play at all these days?*

*I'm afraid you'll block my email or phone number. Please don't.*

Our conversation is a little awkward as we both warm up. We're unsure how to downshift from the basic pleasantries of *How have you been?* and *It's nice to see you.* But a familiar rhythm of thoughtful questions, joking, and laughter takes over soon enough. We meander across several topics. Writing. His relationship. The new car he bought.

"How are things with your partner?" I ask, then quickly add, "Am I allowed to ask that?" I fidget with the lion charm on my necklace.

He laughs. "Yes, you can ask. There's a lot of upheaval and flux there. It consumes my time, my attention, and my willingness to process." I nod; this is what I expected. I've been trying to soothe myself for months with the notion that his lack of contact was about this overwhelm and not about me.

"We're seeing a therapist together," he continues.

"How's that going?"

"It's good, I like talking through things with a third party. It works for me." He seems excited to tell me about couples counseling, and somewhat shocked at how much he enjoys that process.

"See, you're more of a verbal processor than you think," I tease. "How's living together?" I already sense the answer to this one too, but I let him tell me in his own words.

"It's okay. I'm a pretty solitary person, I like my space." My smile catches his attention. "What?" he asks.

"I'm not surprised. I anticipated it would be difficult for you. You're used to having the place to yourself."

He smiles again. "This feels good, seeing you and talking. I'm enjoying this."

"Yeah," I agree, working to keep the edge out of my voice. "This is what I've been asking of you for eight months now."

His dark brown eyes meet mine. "I know. I'm so sorry I wouldn't meet before now. It was never that I didn't want to see you."

I breathe in his apology, let it soak into my skin. "Thank you for saying that. I had my guesses about what kept you away but I didn't know for sure. I was disappointed and hurt by your ongoing silence."

"I'm sorry I caused you pain." He's sincere, I see it on his face, feel his words in my chest.

The sun is out in full force by now; our patch of shade has vanished. When my leg falls asleep from sitting sideways to face him, I ask him to trade places with me on the bench. He stands up, removes his sweatshirt, and sits back down. I fold my other leg up under me, facing him from the other direction as we continue talking.

"You seem good," he says. "I mean with all you've been through…I was worried." His words feel surprisingly sweet as he reaches for a way to reference my sister's death.

"I'm taking really good care of myself," I answer with a shy but confident smile. "I've had to…" I trail off, distracted by remnants of anger at him not supporting me when she died.

"How's your writing going?" he inquires.

"It's great! I'm making progress on that memoir collection I told you about." He looks interested so I keep going. "For my manuscript class we're supposed to write 200 words a day…"

The warmth of his laughter interrupts me, "That shouldn't be hard for you, the way you turn out prose in your emails to me…" I blush at his playful teasing.

We talk about the craft of writing, the ways we both try to intercept the muse as we move through our days. I admit to jotting notes while driving in my car.

"Me, too! Well, I pull over on my bike." His words make me grin.

It's almost time to go. He has somewhere to be and had told me up front that he only had an hour to meet. "So what now?" I ask, anticipating his exit. "I don't want this to be goodbye. I still want to know you."

"I want that too," he says. "But I need a break from contact while I figure things out with my partner. We're still trying to decide whether to stay together and be monogamous, break up, or stay together and see other people."

"That's a lot to sort out," I reflect. "So can we stay in touch on email? I won't overload your inbox, I promise."

"Yes, that works, for now." I watch this consent pass through his brown eyes, see it in the way he nods.

He shifts on the bench, ready to go.

"Is it time to leave?" I ask, pitching my voice calmer than I feel. I don't want this to end.

"Yeah, I should get going." He stands up, so I do too.

He pulls me into another hug. I feel his lips grace the top of my head with a kiss. I could kick him for that! I am both grateful for his sweetness and angry for all the times he's kept it at bay.

"Oh, I almost forgot," I say, reaching into my purse. He looks bewildered as I hand him a paper airplane. "It'll make sense when you read it," I tell him, grinning. After more deliberation than I care to admit, I'd decided to share one piece of writing with him. I figured *One Way Ticket to Whatever* was best presented in the form of a paper airplane.

We walk across the park toward his car, stopping to hug one more time. I don't want to say goodbye. Even though we've decided together this isn't the last time we'll ever see each other, I still don't want to let him out of my sight. But I must.

"Thank you for meeting up today. It's so good to see you." My tone is warm, but docile.

"Yes, thanks for making this happen. It was a good event. I'm glad we did this."

As he walks out of the park, I watch the tall, strong shape of him disappear across the street, then make myself turn around. Relief and desire wrestle within me as I focus my breath.

In some ways I have no more certainty than before; we're still navigating an unclear path. But I am no longer grasping for understanding or answers. I could feel the truth in his embrace, in his hand stroking my hair, in his almost too tender kiss to the crown of my head. The door did not close on our connection; this was not the final, I'll-never-see-you-again, goodbye that I feared.

# TIDBITS

I will feed the breadcrumbs to myself instead of leaving them as a trail of connection and longing between us. I'll still think of you and yearn to tell you things. And I'll promise myself that when that happens, I'll write it anyway, just not to you. I'll give the memory to myself, savor alone the moment of connection that I wish we could share.

I have to expel you as the person in my head that I want to tell everything to. I have to back you out of that position.

Leave it vacant.

Fill it myself.

But it can't be you.

I had already begun to displace you. Seeing you again put you right back into that spot. Listening to your laugh, seeing you smile, feeling your eyes on me and your hands in my hair made it all too real again. I can't let you inhabit that part of my head. Not now, maybe not ever. I can't even hope.

# RELEASE

True to my nature, I arrive early and sit in my car until a minute before I'm expected to arrive. The shades are drawn in the front window of her grey house. The air is just starting to cool from a hot Portland summer day. My pulse races.

At exactly 7:30 p.m. I knock on her door, shivering with nervous excitement. I am so damn ready for this release. She answers the door in worn black jeans and a men's white tank top. Her shoulder-length red hair is pulled back and she smells of spicy, masculine cologne. My heart surges at her attention to these details.

"Come in," she invites, pointing me toward a living room to her right. Deep purple walls, black leather furniture, a small table with kinky implements laid out. I hear her close the front door. And now we begin.

"You're so prompt," she notes, before picking a fight with me about my outfit. After more than a little panic, I had chosen a short black skirt, a tight-fitting, leopard print tank top that had been my sister's, and black, stacked heel sandals, also courtesy of my sister.

She pulls at my tank top, "What is this? Why'd you wear this?"

"It was comfortable, Sir."

"Is that what you're here for, to be comfortable?"

I want to be sassy and tell her that if she'd wanted me to wear something specific, she should have given me instructions. But instead I answer, "No, Sir, that's not why I'm here."

"Damn right. Turn around. Bend over."

"Yes, Sir."

"Your skirt's too long. I'd prefer to be able to almost see your underwear when you bend over."

She knows I'm nervous, does her best to settle me in and offer me reassurance while staying in role. She sits on the black leather couch, orders me to kneel in front of her. "Repeat after me: *While I am in your house, I belong to you...physically, emotionally, and sexually.*"

I say it back to her, my voice shy and tentative.

"*Especially sexually,*" she echoes. I gulp. She adds, "I have this collar for you, but first you have to earn it." A chill of anxious anticipation snakes through me. I have no idea what she has planned.

"Take off your bra, but leave your shirt on." I fumble with the hooks of my bra, my dexterity stolen by nervousness. I'm embarrassed that I can't get it undone.

"Do you need help?" she smirks.

"No, Sir." Stubborn wins out over clumsy. I slide the bra out one side of my tank top.

"Now, pull your shirt up to expose your nipples and play with them in a way that's both pleasurable and painful." My movements are tentative as I follow her instructions.

"Now it's my turn," she grins. Her hands twist and pull at my nipples. I sink into the moment, acclimating to her touch. She places the heavy, chain link collar around my neck and buckles it with a padlock at my throat.

"Take off your shirt. Where are the toys I told you to bring?"

"They're in my bag, Sir."

"Bring them to me and lose the skirt while you're at it. While I look at the toys, I want you to spread that blanket out on the rug."

I hand her two dildos wrapped in colored handkerchiefs and set to work placing the blanket on the rug. She laughs at the hankies, holds up the red one and asks, "Do you know what it means to flag red?"

"Yes, Sir."

"Is fisting something you're interested in?"

"No, Sir."

"Do you know what it means to flag dark green?"

"Yes, Sir."

"Is Daddy play something you're into?"

"It isn't something I've experienced on the receiving end, Sir."

The smile never leaves her face as she issues more commands. "Lie down on the rug, face up, with your head here." She buckles leather cuffs at my wrists, fastens them to eye-bolts in the front corners of a metal platform behind me. This way my arms are extended to either side, slightly above my head. Using her bare hands she begins slapping my tits, thighs, and cunt, slowly increasing in intensity.

She puts nipple clamps on me, first a set that don't fit, then another pair that pinch tighter and stay just fine. "We should get that mouth of yours warmed up," she says, placing a gloved hand at my lips before shoving two fingers in. "Show me what you'll do with my cock." My loud, hungry moans echo in the room. "Let's see what your cunt thinks of that." She pulls her hand out of my mouth and thrusts her fingers between my legs. I'm already wet. She slides my panties off of me and shoves them in my mouth as a gag, something Mr. Lucky always threatened to do, but never did. It's hot, and makes me think of him.

She uses her hand to fuck me and play with my clit, focusing on my pleasure more intently than Mr. Lucky ever had. A wave of sadness crests over me; I tumble between longing for him and reveling in her attention. Lost in my head, unable to respond verbally, I retreat into her touch.

I can't look at her. My eyes close so often that she ties a blindfold on me. "Here, I'll save you the trouble," she quips. At one point, after she blindfolds me, she stops touching me. Still on my back on the floor,

I reach around with my leg, trying to locate her. She laughs at me. "You aren't very subtle when you're naked and bound in front of me. That was fun to watch. Don't worry, I'll tell you when I'm leaving the room."

Even with her encouragement, her taunting me to use my words, I am mostly mute. When I finally choke out that I'm feeling sad, she climbs on top of me and stretches herself out the length of my body. I had told her this would soothe me when I got sad, and it does. It also pushes one of the clamps against my nipple in a way that hurts like fuck. "Oh, does that hurt?" she asks, mocking me. She pulls that clamp off and I jump from the pain. Reaching for the other one, she warns, "This might suck," and yanks it off.

"Damn!" I shriek.

She unbinds my arms and rolls me over onto my belly to fuck me from behind with one of my toys. She refastens my wrists together in front of me, clips them to the post with a carabiner. I writhe and rock as she fucks my cunt and ass. She'd told me earlier that I had to ask permission to orgasm. I want to come but am too overwhelmed. My body can't track all the sensation. The fucking hurts; I don't want it to end. I growl and pant, moan and grunt, but can't speak. "Words, I need your words here," she demands.

Finally I blurt, "It hurts!" and she stops, pulls the toy out and I collapse.

Sadness slides out of me as she sits beside me, stroking my head.

"May I have my hands unbound, please?" She releases them immediately.

"Do you want water?"

"Yes, please. Can I have a tissue, too?" I blow my nose, joke that I'd be a lousy shot with my hands bound. She laughs with me until I go quiet again, adrift in my mind. Words form but I can't voice them. Finally I whisper, "I'm ready to get mad."

Sir sits on the couch beside me, silent. I am lying face down on the rug, my wrists once again bound in front of me. My eyes are covered with the blindfold. "Where'd you go?"

"I'm right here," she says from her seat on the couch.

"I can't feel you, where are you?" Panic amplifies my voice.

She stands up. "I'll be right back, I'm going to get a drink."

This is the cue we agreed on for me to start yelling at her. Her leaving the room mimics the way he walked away from me emotionally in our connection. "Where'd you go? You can't just leave me! Where the fuck did you go?"

"I told you, I'm getting a drink," Sir answers from the other room.

"Goddammit, get back here, you can't just leave me here! You fucking bastard, come back. You can't just walk away from me, you can't just leave me here without telling me what's going on."

I yell and yell until she walks back into the room and then I retreat into silence. She turns around and leaves the room once more so I start yelling again. "Get back here, where'd you go? Don't leave me like this, you can't just walk away!"

She steps back in the room. "What's the big deal? What's all this yelling about? We had a good run, I told you this was just for fun."

"You fucking bastard. You can't say this doesn't matter; you can't say you don't care about me. That's bullshit. You do care, you want this."

She follows my lead, takes the bait I throw at her. "You know I can't care about you like that. You know that wasn't on the table. This was just for fun, we were only playing around, just casual. You're just a plaything for me to use."

I'm hysterical. "That's bullshit. I matter to you. This matters to you. I loved you. I know you don't love me too, but you can't say this doesn't matter to you."

"You know it can't matter to me." These final words from Sir break me. I fall into tears, drop off the edge of an emotional cliff. She comes to lay on top of my back, then frees my hands and lets me curl up beside her. She strokes my hair and kisses my forehead, holds me as I sob.

Once I calm down, we talk for a long while, debriefing, marveling at how well it went. She tells me funny things, like how I stopped yelling when she came into the room and she thought *Oh, that's a neat party trick!* and left again so I could get more out of my system.

I talk about how quiet I'd been and she agrees that I was way less verbal than I'd led her to expect. "I guess I talk a good game," I admit. "I felt tangled in my head and struggled to stay present." She jokes about my outfit, how there wasn't really anything to fight about – it wasn't too slutty or too tame, so she decided my skirt was too long. I gush about how good the physical impact felt, the slapping and the pinching, the rough fucking.

Finally, it's time to say goodbye. I pack up my toys and put my clothes back on. We hug goodbye. I drive the ten minutes home, exhausted and ready for sleep.

# NOT QUITE FINISHED

When I wake up Saturday morning, I know there's been movement in my grief. I've made progress towards closing this dynamic, but it isn't finished yet. I need more.

I text Molly: *Hi. I'm doing well processing last night. Thank you again. I want to step back into that dynamic before cycling my way out. I got a lot of what I was seeking but don't feel complete. Could we scene again tomorrow afternoon? I know that's soon. I'm afraid it isn't ok to want that but I'm pushing past my shame to ask anyway. I don't see myself wanting to play with you in his role ongoing. But at least one more time, please. Sooner than later feels right so I can stop living in this limbo.*

She responds warmly and is willing to meet again the next day. She asks where I want to go when we play again. I email her back with details, feeling like a playwright composing stage direction.

*More pain, please: harder and more slapping, especially my face but also tits, thighs, ass; more hair pulling; more intense input on my back — maybe a flogger (although I love the way you use your hands) with me standing up with my arms bound so I have more room to struggle than I did on my back.*

*The physical impact was excellent, it settled into my body and I felt some of the sadness and rage move through me. I need more of that.*

*And the fucking was fantastic, more of that, too. I want to try to come, which I mostly only do from clitoral stimulation with fingers or a vibrator. I don't want permission to orgasm the first time I ask.*

*If I don't answer your questions or your commands, I want you to stop engaging with me. Tell me you won't touch me again until I tell you what I want or need. I need to push myself to stay present, to tell the truth if I am stuck in my head or my emotions. Even if my answer is "I'm just in the pain" or "I just feel you fucking me" I have to answer, or you stop. This will help me not disappear and reinforce using my voice. I spoke up to orchestrate getting to play with you, creating this outlet for myself. I need to use my words more when I'm there too; I need to not hide.*

I'm afraid of directing too much but Molly assures me it's necessary. "We'll be flexible in scene, but I need this much detail in order to support you in these specific dynamics."

The main thing I need to replay is the ending. I have to hear myself end Mr. Lucky's power over me. I script it with precision but leave enough space for us to improvise as needed.

# FINALE

By Sunday afternoon, when I arrive at her place again, I am ready to finish this. The scene unfolds just the way I intend, with more intense sensation and a slightly rougher tone on her part. And I use my voice. Only once do I go quiet enough for her to take her hands off me, and I recover quickly. The threat of not having her touch is potent enough to keep me answering her questions.

When I'm ready for the finale I designed, she orders me to sit on the leather bench facing her. She binds my arms behind my back and tells me to spread my legs. She sits across from me on the couch, teasing me. "What a slutty whore you are, spread open for me to use in any way I want. Such a sexy plaything…" She stands up and walks into the next room where I can't see her. As I watch her disappear, I feel anger rise to my throat.

I yell all the same things, "You can't just walk away! What's going on? You can't just not tell me what's going on? Sir! Where are you? Don't do this!"

After several minutes of my rant, she storms back into the room and gets in my face. "What do you want, bitch? What do you want from me?" Sir slaps me across the face. I don't flinch.

"Is that the best you can do?" I taunt her.

She slaps me harder.

"I want you to tell me the truth. Admit that you want this, but you can't do it, you need to disengage. Don't just walk away, tell me the fucking truth!"

Without answering me, she turns around and walks out of my line of sight. I come undone. "Where the fuck did you go? You fucking bastard, don't walk away from me. Answer me, tell me the goddamned truth!" I wear myself out yelling into the empty room.

Her silence fills the space until I can hardly breathe. I feel a shift in my center, notice my emotion change from rage to resilience. "Come back here. Take this collar off of me."

She steps out from behind a curtain in the other room, walks toward me without a word. Her eyes meet mine, steely and cold. I glare back at her, feel the chill of his cool demeanor staring back at me. As she reaches to unbuckle the collar, I breathe into my full, clear voice. "I don't belong to you anymore. I'm not yours. Goodbye, Sir."

She slips the collar off my neck and walks away. I spy her peeking at me from the other room, waiting to see how I'll respond. Neither of us expect the grin on my face, or the easy laughter of relief that spills from me.

What I feel more than anything is that it worked. I wanted to replace his power over me with my own strength. I needed to return to myself. And I have.

I invite Molly back in and she releases my hands. I curl into her as we come down from the scene. I am exhausted, relieved, and complete. My closing words echo in my head:

*I don't belong to you anymore. I'm not yours.*

# ABOUT THE AUTHOR

Photo by Natasha Komoda

Meg Weber writes memoir about sex, grief, love, family, therapy, and tangled relationships. Meg's writing gives voice to the ways her life continues to unfold outside the boundaries prescribed for her. She is a queer mental health therapist who specializes in gender and sexuality, an adjunct instructor in counselor education, and a clinical supervisor. She lives in her hometown of Portland, Oregon with her teenager and their labradoodle named Portland.

CPSIA information can be obtained
at www.ICGtesting.com
Printed in the USA
BVHW070718040221
599237BV00004B/795